Requests as Reasons

Requests as Reasons

A Philosophical Account

Peter Schaber

BLOOMSBURY ACADEMIC
NEW YORK • LONDON • OXFORD • NEW DELHI • SYDNEY

BLOOMSBURY ACADEMIC
Bloomsbury Publishing Inc, 1359 Broadway, New York, NY 10018, USA
Bloomsbury Publishing Plc, 50 Bedford Square, London, WC1B 3DP, UK
Bloomsbury Publishing Ireland, 29 Earlsfort Terrace, Dublin 2, D02 AY28, Ireland

First published in the United States of America 2026

A catalog record for this book is available from the Library of Congress.

ISBN: HB: 978-1-6669-5536-1
ePDF: 979-8-216-26063-9
eBook: 978-1-9787-6368-5

Typeset by Newgen KnowledgeWorks Pvt. Ltd., Chennai, India

For product safety related questions contact productsafety@bloomsbury.com.

To find out more about our authors and books visit www.bloomsbury.com and sign up for our newsletters.

Contents

Acknowledgments

I owe my gratitude to many colleagues and friends, without whom this book could not have been written. I am especially thankful to the participants of the workshops on normative power in Oxford and Berlin for their thoughtful questions and critiques. My sincere thanks go to Francis Cheneval for our discussions on practical authority and to Thomas Schmidt for his insights into what it takes to issue binding orders and the relationship between oughts and reasons. I am deeply grateful to Felix Koch for countless insightful conversations on normative powers. I also greatly benefited from long and intense discussions with Anna Goppel on various topics of the manuscript. The book would not have been possible without the countless exchanges I had with Stefan Riedener on the nature and normativity of requests. I am especially thankful to Susanne Boshammer for her illuminating discussions and unwavering encouragement.

I would like to thank the participants of the manuscript workshop: Andreas Müller for organizing it and for his valuable feedback; Lukas Naegeli for his critical observations; and Susanne Boshammer, Micha Gläser, Dan Khokhar, Jennifer Page, and Daniel Weltman for their detailed feedback on the entire manuscript. Their feedback was invaluable. I am also grateful to an anonymous reviewer whose comments significantly improved the final version.

Special thanks go to Jana Hodges Kluck, who encouraged me to develop the ideas from my article "The Reason-Giving Force of Requests" (*Ethical Theory and Moral Practice*, 2021) into a book-length study. Her support and belief in the project meant a great deal.

Finally, I thank my children, Denis and Jannick, for their love, and Nina, whose constant encouragement helped me see this book through to the end.

Introduction

0.1 Requests as Reasons

We are all familiar with the practice of making requests. We ask others for favors, and others ask favors of us. It is hard to imagine a society where this practice is unknown, as it forms a fundamental part of our daily interactions. Consider common examples: "Could you please open the door for me?" or "Could you please be quiet now?" Often, we comply with such requests, fulfilling what is asked of us. At other times, we decline, sometimes without much thought or consideration.

The act of making requests raises important normative questions: Should requests always be honored? Under what circumstances should they be honored? When is it permissible to turn them down? And when may or should they be refused outright? Suppose your neighbor asks you to help her move house. Should you comply with her request? Can you turn it down? Would it be wrong to refuse? Are you at least obliged to consider her request? What if your friend asked you to move house? Would her request be more important than the one your neighbor made? Might some requests be dismissed without any thought? Additionally, we are sometimes unsure whether it is appropriate to ask someone to do something for us. Is it acceptable to ask a colleague I have never met to read my 300-page manuscript? Would it be appropriate to ask my neighbor to talk to my wife about a personal issue? The practice of making requests raises a variety of normative issues, which will be explored in this book on requests as reasons.

There is also the question of what requests are. What exactly do we do when we make a request? For example, you ask your colleague if she could read your paper. One view is that, in making this request, you are informing your colleague that you want her to read your paper. The request might draw her attention to something she has a reason to do. She may have a reason to do what you want her to do. Or she may have a reason to read your paper because she works on the same topic, or because she is interested in learning about your position and arguments.

However, another view suggests that making a request is not merely about informing the *requestee* (the person who receives the request) of your desire. While your request does communicate that you have this desire, it also goes further. According to Joseph Raz, requests are made to create reasons for the requestee to act. Your request for your colleague to read your paper is intended to serve as a reason for her to do so. Raz writes:

> A person who makes a request intends his making the request to be a reason for the addressee to comply with. He hopes no doubt that his request will be a conclusive reason, but he does not intend it to be an exclusionary reason. (Raz 1975, 83)

It is important to note that, on this view, the *requester* (the person who makes the request) wants to create a reason for the requestee to comply with the request. It does not have to be a reason that prevails over all other reasons applying to the requestee when the request is made. But the request is supposed to be a *pro tanto reason* for the requestee to do as requested. A pro tanto reason must be distinguished from an all-things-considered reason for action. If you have an all-things-considered reason to φ, you ought to φ. By contrast, if you have a pro tanto reason to φ, there is something that speaks in favor of φ-ing. If the pro tanto reason to φ is not outweighed or defeated by other reasons, you may φ, and in certain cases, you ought to φ. A pro tanto reason to do x is a consideration that speaks in favor of doing x.

The reason created by the request is an additional reason to the request-independent reasons that might already exist for the addressee to do as requested. I will argue that by making a request you communicate the intention to create a reason for the addressee. By contrast, by issuing an order you communicate the intention to impose a duty on the addressee, not just a reason.

What are requests? First, it is not always easy to identify requests. What is presented as a request is often nothing more than an order. For example, if an employer asks an employee whether she would be ready to write a letter, it might be framed as a request. However, given the hierarchical relationship at the workplace, it is actually an order to write the letter. The employee understands she is obliged to write the letter and recognizes that the employer, in an attempt to be polite, has framed the order as a request.

Sometimes, it is unclear whether a particular speech act is a request or merely the expression of a wish. Consider the statement, "I'd be happy if you read my paper." This could be interpreted as a request, but it may also be an expression of a wish. To determine whether it is a request or a wish, one must be familiar with the context of the utterance, understand how the speech act was intended, and possibly anticipate how the speaker would react if the paper is not read. To identify whether something is a request, you need to have an understanding of what constitutes a request. Is it simply information about what you want someone to do for you, or is it an attempt to create a reason for the addressee to act by making the request?

Following an epistemic account of requests, a request informs the requestees that the requester wants them to do or omit something. According to this view, a request simply expresses a desire that the requester has, which has a specific object: namely, the requestee's doing or omitting something. In contrast, the alternative view I favor holds that requests do more than merely inform the requestees of the requester's desire. Instead, requests are acts aimed at bringing about a normative change. When you make a request, you are communicating the intention to create a reason for the requestee to comply with your request. If the requester genuinely intends to create such a reason, the request is sincere. If the requester merely pretends to have this intention, the request is insincere.

As concerns the normativity of requests, I argue in this book that requests can sometimes create reasons for action and sometimes obligations. I will refer to this as the normative force of requests. I will show how requests sometimes create reasons and sometimes obligations. The epistemic view holds that by informing the requestees of what the requester desires, the requester may draw the requestee's attention to an already existing reason to comply with the request. In contrast, I argue that requests themselves possess normative force if certain conditions are met. Requests create reasons for the requestee to honor if and only if it is good to take the request as a reason for action. It is good to treat a request as a reason for action when it is good to comply with the request because it was made. However, requests create reasons only if the requested act is good or at least not sufficiently bad. If it is indeed good to treat a request as a reason, and there is no sufficiently strong reason not to honor the request (none strong enough to outweigh the reason provided by the request), then a normative principle exists in the following form: "If and because A asks B to do x, B has a reason to do x."

I will argue that in some cases, requests do not merely create reasons but impose obligations. Requests can create obligations even though the requester does not intend to impose an obligation on the requestee, unlike in the case of an order, where the prescriber communicates the intention to impose an obligation on the addressee of the order. Whether a request creates reasons or obligations is determined by request norms, which can be framed as follows: "If and because A asks B to do x, B has a reason to do x." The request might trigger an obligation, thus imposing an obligation on B to honor the request: "If and because A asks B to do x, B is obliged to do x." Alternatively, the reason might not trigger an obligation, and thus B not obliged to honor the request. Whether B has a reason or an obligation depends on the norms governing the relationship between the requester and the requestee. For example, a request from a friend might create an obligation to comply, while a request from a stranger might only provide a reason to comply. Or so I will argue.

I will also argue that not all requests lead to a normative change. Some requests fail to bring about a normative change. For instance, if A asks B to do x, there may be no request norm of the form: "If and because A asks B to do x, B has a reason to do x." Such a norm does not exist if it is inappropriate or wrong to treat the request as a reason. This could be the case for various reasons: it might be wrong to grant the favor being asked, or it might be wrong for the requested act to be performed because the requestee was asked to do so.

I also argue that the requester might be disappointed if the request is turned down, either because she hoped the requestee would comply or because she feels let down by the requestee's failure to meet an ideal, such as being a good friend or colleague. If the requestee is obliged to comply, the requester might be entitled to complain about non-compliance or the request not being considered.

Even though requests may sometimes create obligations, they differ from orders. When someone makes a request, she communicates the intention to create a reason, leaving it up to the requestee to comply. In contrast, an order conveys the prescriber's intention to impose an obligation on the addressee, not leaving it up to her to comply. The addressee is not supposed to weigh the pros and cons. By contrast, the requestee is permitted to weigh all relevant reasons for and against compliance in the given situation. Or so I will argue.

0.2 The Structure of the Book

This is how the book is structured, chapter by chapter. Chapter 1 discusses two views on requests—epistemic and normative. It explores how requests either track reasons (epistemic view) or create reasons (normative view), with the chapter arguing that requests aim to create reasons and that the reason-giving force of requests can be explained by request norms. Chapter 2 explains what request norms are and debates whether they should be understood as conventions, as established norms, or as practice-independent norms. The chapter argues that a request norm exists if it is good or at least not sufficiently bad to perform the requested act and if it is good to take the request as a reason for action.

Chapter 3 examines how requests create reasons and obligations and the importance of the normative structure of the relationship between requester and requestee. Chapter 4 compares requests and orders, discussing the ability to give binding orders. It also explains how order norms are justified, how they differ from request norms, and how obligations are created differently by orders. Chapter 5 compares requesting and begging, arguing that begging is not inherently demeaning and can create reasons for action similar to requests.

Chapter 6 examines situations in which requests fail to bring about normative change, for example, when they conflict with the kind of relationship the requestee wants to have with the requester, wrong the requestee, or are accompanied by threats. It also shows how deception affects the normative force of requests. Chapter 7 examines the normativity of turning down requests, exploring when such refusals are justified and when requesters are justified in being disappointed or complaining about a refusal. Chapter 8 provides a summary of the main points covered throughout the book.

1

The Normative View

We are able to change the rights and obligations we have toward each other by means of certain actions. We can do this by promising, by consenting, by giving an order, or by making demands. By promising you put yourself under an obligation. By giving orders you put—given that you have the required authority—another person under an obligation. By consenting you release the other person from an obligation toward you. We also seem to change the reasons for actions other people have by making requests. Consider the following example: A and B have dinner together. A asks B to pass the salt. B passes the salt. B acts for a reason. B has a reason to pass the salt because A wants B to pass the salt. Or alternatively, one might say, B has a reason to pass the salt because she was asked to do so. The scenario can be described in two different ways. In this chapter, I will examine these two views, the epistemic and the normative view, each of which considers one description superior to the other.

A's request provides B with a reason to act on both accounts. But how exactly do requests provide us with reasons? There are two views here, an *epistemic* and a *normative* view. On the epistemic view requests track reasons, they do not create reasons (Weltman 2023; see also Laskowski and Silver 2021). A's request tracks a reason to act for B because A informs B that she wants her to pass the salt. A's desire that B pass the salt is—one might say—a reason to do so. Thus, A's request informs B that B has a reason to pass the salt. The request tracks the reason that obtains independently of A asking B to pass the salt. On this view, requests have a purely epistemic function to provide us access to reasons that apply to us. By contrast, on the normative view, requests create reasons for action (Raz 1975; Enoch 2011; Lewis 2018; Schaber 2021). B has a reason to pass the salt because A asked B to do so. It is the act of asking B to pass the salt that creates a reason for B to pass the salt. Some go further and argue that requests create obligations (Cupit 1994; Gläser 2019). B is under an obligation to pass the salt because she has been asked by A to do so. On both accounts requests change the normative situations. The question is: Are requests only tracking reasons? Or are they able to create reasons or even obligations? This is the question this chapter will deal with.

1.1 Overview

In this chapter, I will argue that, by making a request, one communicates an intention to change the normative situation in a specific way. A person making a request seeks to motivate the requestee to act by creating a reason to do so. For instance, if A asks B to pass the salt, A communicates the intention that her request itself serves as a reason for B to comply. This is what I call the "normative view of requests." On this view, we sometimes create reasons and sometimes obligations by asking others to do us a favor. On the epistemic view, A's desire gives B a reason to comply. A's request tracks this reason by informing B that A wants B to do her a favor. However, the request itself has no normative force, it rather tracks reasons that already exist, provided that A's desire does give B a reason to act.

I will argue in this chapter that while the request informs B of A's desire, the act of asking creates an additional reason for action if certain conditions are met. B could be aware of A's desire without being explicitly asked. If A's desire provided B with a reason for action, no request would be necessary in such a case. However, A might desire that B pass the salt without actually asking B to do so. Even though she has this desire, she does not want to request B to pass the salt. It makes sense to say, "I would like you to do x, but I will not ask you to do it." This statement only makes sense if the request does more than merely inform the requestee about the requester's desire. It makes sense because when A makes the request, she communicates an intention to create a reason: "I want my request to be a reason for you to pass the salt." This aligns with the fact that we understand requests as reasons for action. We recognize them as such when we say, "I did x because I was asked to do x." The act of requesting is often understood as the reason for complying with the request.

But how do requests create reasons? The reason-giving force of requests can be explained by reference to request norms. Request norms have the form "If and because A asks B to do x, B has a reason to do x." A request creates a reason for action when it falls under a request norm. For example, there is a request norm stating that if A asks B to pass the salt, B has a reason to comply. However, not all requests create reasons. If A asks B to kill C, no reason to do as requested is created. There is no request norm stating, "If A asks B to kill C, B has a reason to do so." For a request norm to exist, the requested action must meet specific conditions: it should be pro tanto good or at least not sufficiently bad to perform the requested act and good to take the request as a reason. Passing the salt satisfies these conditions, whereas killing someone does not. Honoring such a request might serve the requester's interest, but it would be bad overall.

As I will argue, *a request norm of the form, "If A asks B to do x, B has a reason to do x," holds if and only if it is good or at least not sufficiently bad to do x, and it is good to take the request as a reason for action.* It is a necessary condition for a request to be a reason to be honored that the requested act is good or not sufficiently bad.

Requests are intended to motivate requestees to do what the requesters want them to do. There are, however, alternative ways to achieve this, such as through threats ("I will harm you if you don't pass me the salt"), incentives ("I'll buy you a drink if you pass me the salt"), orders ("As your superior, I'm telling you to pass the salt"), or even deception ("Your boss will be impressed if she sees you passing the salt"). *Requests are attempts to get others to do something without relying on deception, coercion, or personal incentives. Requests are attempts to get others to do something out of respect for the reasons-giving authority of the requester.*

Let us now explore these points in greater detail. The chapter has eight parts. The first part presents the epistemic view of requests. The second part tells us what the epistemic view takes to be the nature of requests and how making a request should be understood. The third part shows the two difficulties the epistemic view faces and why it should be replaced by a normative view. The fourth part clarifies what distinguishes a request from a wish. The fifth part explains the nature of the normative view of requests. The sixth part shows why we need requests and why the interests they serve cannot be served by other means. The seventh part addresses two objections to the normative view of requests, and the eighth part concludes.

1.2 The Epistemic View

David Weltman defends an epistemic account of the normativity of requests (Weltman 2022, 2023).[1] He argues that requests have an epistemic function in providing reasons for action by revealing facts that give us reasons to act. According to his view, when A requests that B pass the salt, this request communicates to B that A has a desire for the salt to be passed. This fact—that A wants the salt to be passed—can serve as a reason for B to honor the request. In other words, B might have a reason to pass the salt simply because A desires it. Weltman suggests that A's request can thus track a reason B has to act, which is provided by A's desire for the salt. Weltman writes:

> When I request that you pass the salt, this gives you a reason to pass the salt because it informs you that I want the salt. This might make it the case that your objective reason to give me the salt I want also becomes a subjective reason to give me the salt I want [if this objective reason in fact exists]. The objective reason came into existence before I requested that you pass the salt: as soon as I wanted you to pass the salt, it existed. (Weltman 2023, 2)

If A's desire to get the salt is a reason for B to pass the salt, then this reason existed before B was asked by A to pass the salt. The reason was made known to B through A's request. Weltman views this reason as an objective reason, which exists independently of A's request. A's request informs B of A's desire. A is making the request because she wants B to pass the salt. The objective reason should then become a subjective reason for B to comply with A's request—a reason that B acts on if she decides to pass the salt. When requests track reasons for action, the requestee learns about the objective reason through the request. This is the case when the request draws the requestee's attention to a reason-giving fact. The reason for the requestee to comply might be due to the requester's desire or because it is beneficial for the requester to get the salt. If B passes the salt, A will either get what she wants or receive something that is good for her.

However, a requester might also communicate a desire to the requestee without genuinely having this desire. Such requests are insincere and lead the addressees to mistakenly believe that the requester genuinely wants them to act in a certain way. Weltman argues that insincere requests do not properly track reasons. In such cases, the requestee would only have an apparent reason to act. For example, B would have an apparent reason to pass the salt if A did not actually want her to do so. As Weltman puts it,

> When I insincerely request the salt, you mistakenly believe I want the salt … the request is not "really normative" if by "really" normative we mean that the request tells you about your objective normative domain … It is apparently normative … and apparent normativity is the only normativity we can act on. (Weltman 2023, 11).

Insincere requests do not track objective reasons. They provide the requestees with subjective reasons they might act on. In such cases, they perform acts they do not have reasons to perform.

It is important to note that, on the epistemic account, requests do not create reasons. The reason for B to pass the salt existed before the request was made. Thus, requests, on this account, lack normative force. Instead, as Weltman states, requests have a "normatively valuable result" (Weltman 2023, 24) by highlighting reasons that already apply to the requestee. These reasons are not created by the requests, they are rather independent of them.

On Weltman's account, requests provide—in addition to informing the requestee of the desires the requester has—evidence for something else. They indicate the requester's consent to the requestee performing the act requested. That is, they serve as expressions of consent (Weltman 2023, 17). For example, when A asks B to pass the salt, A is indicating that B has her permission to do so. A's request serves as evidence of her consent, informing B that A has consented to B passing the salt and thus permitted B to do so.

> We can take requests to constitute *evidence* of consent because issuing a request can itself constitute consent. Thus, if I request that you X, this constitutes evidence that I consent to you Xing. (Weltman 2023, 17)

I understand "constituting consent" to mean that by making a request, one consents to the requested act. For example, if A asks B to attend her party, A thereby consents to B's attendance. In this way, A's request functions as a waiver of a right she might otherwise hold against B. However, this interpretation conflicts with the epistemic view. According to that view, making a request is not an exercise of a normative power, it neither creates reasons nor waives rights. Consequently, requests cannot grant permission. Requests merely provide evidence that the requester consents to the requestee performing the requested act. When you ask someone to do something, you are informing the requestee that consent has been given to perform the act in question.

Weltman argues further that the epistemic account has the advantage of not being obliged to posit a special sort of normativity for requests. The epistemic account is simpler than alternative theories and should therefore be preferred. It is simpler because it explains why requests are reason-giving without invoking a special reason-creating force. Weltman writes:

> We need not posit a special sort of normativity for requests. If we can account for the normative features of the world without complicating our picture of normativity, this is nice. … [E]very account of requests must *also* say that requests can be normative in the way the epistemic account says they are normative, because certainly requests *sometimes* give reasons merely by revealing information. So, since everyone already admits the epistemic account is operating, it is simpler if we can explain requests entirely by adverting to that account. (Weltman 2023, 26)

The epistemic account, according to Weltman, can explain everything necessary regarding the normativity of requests. It accounts for our understanding of requests as providing reasons. On his view, this explanation of the normativity of requests is sufficient and does not require us to consider additional reasons beyond those we are already familiar with, reasons that are provided by the requester's desires.

1.3 The Nature of Requests

Should we accept the epistemic account of requests? This account faces two difficulties. First, it can't explain (a) why expressing a desire is not the sa as making a request, and (b) why we treat requests as reasons for action. By contrast, the view I will call the normative view accounts for both (a) and (b).

Thus, we should reject the epistemic view of requests for two reasons. First, it is based on a mistaken understanding of what requests are, as shown by its inability to account for statements like "I would like you to do X, but I will not ask you to do so," and by the fact that requests are not merely understood as conveying information. Second, it fails to explain why requests often serve as reasons for action, as illustrated by the example: "I am helping you move house because you asked me to do so."

Regarding the first point (a): According to the epistemic view, requests merely inform the requestee that the requester wants something done or omitted. By doing so, requests might draw the requestee's attention to reasons for complying. However, requests are not simply about informing the requestee of the requester's desires. A person makes a request by performing a communicative act that not only informs the requestee of their desire for them to act in a certain way. Raz rightly puts it:

> It would be wrong to regard requests as mere communication of information that the speaker … needs or wants something and that the speaker wants the addressee to help in getting it. Although every request at least implies such information, it is possible to communicate the information without requesting. (Raz 1975, 83)

You might inform someone that you want her to do something, and you could add that you will not ask her to do it: "I would be happy if you read my paper but I will not ask you to do it." This sentence makes perfect sense. Making a request is thus more than merely informing someone of your desire. A request aims to provide the other person with a reason to act as requested, to do what the requester wants them to do because they were asked to do so.

As Raz writes,

> A person who makes a request intends his making the request to be a reason for the recipient to comply with it. (Raz 1975, 83)[2]

If you ask another person to do x you want your request to be a *reason* for the requestee to do as requested. The requester does not need to actually intend to eate a reason; she could merely pretend to have such an intention. However, by making a request, she communicates the intention to create a reason, even if she does not genuinely have that intention.

Thus, this is then what I take requests to be (R):

> (R) A person who makes a request communicates her intention to give the requestee a reason to do as requested.

Why should we accept (R)? Consider the salt example again. B might know that A wants her to pass the salt without having been asked by A to do so. If requesting was all about informing the requestee that you want her to do something, A did not have to ask B to pass the salt if A knew that B knew that she wanted her to pass the salt. However, it makes sense to ask B to do so. (R) explains, as Raz puts it, "why one might request even when one knows that the other person knows of one's need and of one's desire for help" (Raz 1986, 37).[3]

In addition, requests are not understood as mere information about our desires. Consider the following example: A thirteen-year-old named John tells his parents that he wants them to buy him an ice cream. They are displeased with how he expresses this. "How do we put this?" they respond. Sensing their disapproval, John rephrases his statement: "Could you please buy me an ice cream?" This is now understood as a request. The word *please* signals that he is not simply conveying a desire but offering a reason to be considered. It highlights that the decision ultimately lies with his parents, underscoring their authority and discretion in responding to his request.

Concerning the second point (b): It holds that we take requests to be reasons for action. "I read your paper, because you asked me to read it." The explanation of my act refers to your request as a reason. Your request was my reason to read your paper. I could say "I would not have read it if you had not asked me to read it. I knew that you wanted me to read it, but I only read it because you asked me to do so." We take requests as reasons for action. The epistemic view has difficulty accounting for this practice. On that view, requests are not reasons for action. You can only take the requester's desire as a reason to comply and act as requested because they want you to.

The requestee can do as requested because she was asked to do so. She can also do as requested for other reasons. My colleague might read my paper because I asked her to, or she might read it because she works on the same topic and wants to understand my thoughts and arguments. Thus, requests can be complied with for two different kinds of reasons: for request-dependent reasons (RDR) and for request-independent reasons (RIR):

> (RDR) Request-dependent reasons are those reasons to do what has been requested that are created by one's being asked to do so.[4]
>
> (RIR) Request-independent reasons are those reasons to do what has been requested that exist independently of having been asked to do so.

The requester gets what she wants if the requestee does what the requester wants her to do. The requester can get what she wants for request-dependent as well as for request-independent reasons. In both cases she gets what she wants.

If the requestee does what she is asked to do because she was asked to do it, she is said to comply with the request. If she does it for RIR, she conforms to the request. I will use the expression "honoring a request" to encompass both cases, whether the requestee acts for RDR and RIR.

We should note here that we can also ask someone for something without having a desire that the requestee will comply and without having the intention to create a reason for the requestee to comply with the request. Take the case of A asking B to do x. A could do this simply out of politeness, that is, because A knows that B would be offended if she did not ask her. A might hope that her request will be turned down by B. The question is: Did A make a request? You do not make a request if you do not represent yourself as having an intention to create a reason and a desire that the other person acts on it. But you can represent yourself as having the intention to create a reason for the requestee without actually having it. Then you are making a request. A makes a request because she wants to be polite. If B learns that A does not want to create a reason for her, she will no longer take his request as a reason for her to read his draft. However, you make a request if you communicate that you want someone else to do something, and your request to be a reason to do it. You can communicate this without having the intention to create a reason and a desire that the other person acts accordingly. It would be an insincere request, lacking normative force. As long as the requestee believes it to be sincere, she may have reason to honor it. But once she realizes the requester had no intention of giving her a reason to act, she should no longer treat the request as providing one.

It is also important to note that a request does not need uptake by the requestee to be considered a request. Consider this case. John writes Jill an email asking Jill to read his draft. He has made a request by writing the email. Jill might not read the email, still, he would have asked her to read his draft. He makes a request if he intentionally communicates that he wants Jill to read his draft. Thus, he made a request, regardless of whether Jill had read his email.

You can communicate your intention to create a reason for another person, but your request might mistakenly be interpreted as an order. Consider this. Joe's boss asks him to write a letter. Against the background of their hierarchical relation Joe takes the speech-act as an order, even though it was not meant as an order but rather as a request. It is a request if the boss' speech act was meant to be a reason to write the letter and not as an obligation-imposing order. Joe might be justified in taking the speech act as an order ("it sounded like an order, and not to forget, she is my boss"). However, it is not an order if it was not meant as an order but rather as a request. Thus, A is requesting B to do x, if and only if A communicates that she wants B to do x and intends her request to be a reason for B to do so.

1.4 Requests and Wishes

Requests differ from expressed wishes. When you say "I wish that you called me tonight," you are not making a request, you only express a wish. According to Weltman, both requests and wishes inform the addressee about something the requester and the one who expresses the wish want the addressee to do, potentially drawing their attention to reasons for action. The requestee and the addressee of a wish may each have reasons to honor what is expressed. On Weltman's view requests and wishes do not differ concerning their normative force. They both try to draw the addressee's attention to reasons that apply to her. They only differ regarding the information they convey. When you request someone to call you tonight, you indicate to the requestee that the act is more important to you than if you had merely expressed a wish to be called. Weltman writes:

> So for instance if I request that you X rather than wish that you X, this typically implies that I care more that you X than would have been implied if I had chosen to wish instead. (Weltman 2022, 20)

This may well hold in typical cases of requesting and wishing. The reason a requestee has to honor a request is thus generally stronger than the reason to honor a wish.

Requests, therefore, increase the likelihood of getting the requestee to act in the desired way.[5] However, unlike Weltman, I believe that requests and wishes also differ in their normative force. As I mentioned earlier, when you make a request, you communicate the intention to provide the requestee with a reason to comply. In contrast, wishes are not meant to provide others with reasons for action. For instance, if you wish that I call you tonight, you do not expect me to do so simply because of your wish. Wishes are not intended to influence others' behavior. While they might influence behavior if expressed, that is not their purpose.

Take Weltman's example: "I wish you would wear something nice tonight" (Weltman 2022, 21). I would be pleased if you wore something nice tonight, but I do not want you to do it just to make me happy. I do not consider my pleasure as a reason for you to act accordingly. Instead, I would want you to do it based on the reasons you have for wearing something nice. Since I do not intend my wish to serve as a reason for you, it makes sense for me not to communicate it. Expressing a wish could be misconstrued as a request and thus as an attempt to provide a reason for action. By making a request, you ordinarily aim to create a reason for the addressee to act. By expressing a wish, you merely inform others of a desire, which should not be taken as a reason for compliance. This is why wishes are often left unspoken. When we express them, they might easily be interpreted as requests, and thus as attempts to create reasons. If it is a wish rather than a request, then it is not intended to serve as a reason for the addressee to act accordingly. From the wisher's perspective, it would be good if the addressee fulfilled the wish, but not something she ought to do because the wish was expressed. As Weltman rightly puts it,

> Social conventions in contemporary American society (which I use as my example because I am most familiar with it) dictate that if one *merely* wishes that someone else do something, one typically ought to keep this to oneself. Thus, if one expresses a "wish," it is taken to constitute a request, albeit one expressed via the locution of a wish. (Weltman 2022, 21)

Unlike wishes, requests do not merely inform others about your desires. Requests, unlike wishes, are intended to provide reasons for the addressee to act. The epistemic view cannot account for the differing normative force between requests and wishes. "I would be happy if you did x" is the expression of a wish. Expressions of wishes are not intended to create reasons for action. This is what distinguishes them from requests. Unlike requests, they have no normative force. Sentences like "I would be happy if you did x" have normative force only if they are rightly understood as requests.

1.5 The Normative View

On the normative view of requests, requests create reasons for action, and, as we will see, sometimes also obligations. They create *normative reasons* for action. A normative reason to do something is—as Scanlon puts it—"a consideration that counts in favor of (doing) it" (Scanlon 1998, 17). If you have a reason to do x something speaks in favor of doing x. *Normative reasons* for action are not the same thing as motivating reasons. You might do x for reasons that are not the reasons speaking in favor of doing x. You might, for instance, do me a favor not because I asked you or because it is good for me, but rather because you want to impress a friend of mine. My request and the fact that doing x is good for me are reasons to honor my request, to impress my friend, the reason why you do it.

On the normative view, the act of requesting sometimes creates a reason in favor of honoring the request. Take the salt example. A's request to pass the salt is a reason for B to do so. A's desire to get the salt may also be a reason to pass the salt. A's request, however, creates an additional reason to do so. B may pass the salt because B has been asked to do so. This reason would not exist if A had not made the request. A's request creates a reason to comply. Consider this: A does not ask B to pass the salt, but B knows that A wants the salt. In such a case, B would not know whether she should pass the salt, and A might want to get it herself. Once A makes the request, B knows that A wants her to act accordingly. A's request then provides B with the reason to do so.

Weltman argues that the epistemic view can explain why a request "please do x" is required, even if the requestee already knew that the requester wants her to do x. Doing x might be impermissible and has to be made permissible by the agent who wants the requestee to do x. Requests provide the requestees with evidence that the requester has given consent. The request, Weltman writes, "alters the normative situation, because my request constitutes consent, and consent modifies the situation ... So for instance when I request you to pass the salt, this also constitutes my consent that you pass the salt (and evidence of my consent that you pass the salt)" (Weltman 2023, 17). You might want me to do x, but you are not willing to give me permission to do so.[6] I need your consent to be allowed to do x. The request provides evidence that the latter is the case.

Are acts of request required as expressions of consent? What happens when we consent? Valid consent changes the normative situation by releasing the consent-receiver from an obligation not to act in a certain way (Hurd 1996, Hurd 2018). I might be under an obligation not to do x unless you consent. Your consent to my doing x releases me from this obligation and makes it the case that I will not wrong you by doing x.

Weltman argues that someone is released from an obligation when a request is made. Specifically, when you ask me to do *x*, I am released from an obligation I would otherwise have not to do x. This is why requests must be made; the mere expression of a desire would not be enough because you might want me to do x without consenting to my doing x. If you ask me to x, you also consent to my doing x.

Is this an explanation of why requests are required, even when the requestee is already aware of the requester's desires? Are requests necessary to inform the requestee that the requester has given consent? I do not think so, for two reasons: (a) Not all requests can only be honored if they are consented to. (b) In cases where the requestee must know that consent has been given, the information must come from consent itself, not from the request.

Regarding (a), Weltman argues that requests are required to provide the requestee with evidence of consent. However, this applies only to consent-requiring acts, not to all acts one might be asked to perform. Consider the salt case again: A does not ask B to pass the salt, but B assumes A might need it and passes the salt. B would not thereby wrong A. Passing the salt is not a consent-requiring act. B may pass the salt without A's consent. A's asking B to pass the salt is thus required for other reasons, not to permit B, but rather to create a reason for B to pass the salt, one that B would not have had if A had not made the request.

Regarding (b), even if all requested acts were consent-requiring acts, requests would not be required to provide someone with the information they need to do what the requester wants them to do. To get B to pass the salt, A should inform B that she wants her to do so and consent to her doing it. A could simply say, "I want the salt and consent to you passing it to me." In this case, A's request would not be necessary. Thus, the epistemic view cannot explain why requests are required to get others to do what we want them to do.

On the normative view, requests are intended to serve as reasons for complying with them. However, as I have argued, the reason created by a request might not always play a role in explaining the requestee's compliance with it. Requestees can either comply with or conform to requests. They *comply* with a request if they act as requested because they were asked to do so. They *conform* to a request if they act as requested for reasons independent of the request itself. For example, Jill might read John's paper not because he asked her to, but because she is interested in what he wrote on a topic that aligns with her own research. In this case, Jill is not complying with John's request but rather conforming to it. The request may not serve as a motivating reason for compliance, but it would still be a normative reason to act as requested.

1.6 Request Norms

The way requests create reasons takes a distinctive form. David Enoch calls this reason-giving in a "robust sense" (Enoch 2011, 1). Enoch thinks that this form of reason-giving has to be distinguished from a non-robust form of reason-giving. Consider one of Enoch's example (Enoch 2011, 3): A grocer demands a higher price for his milk. The price change alters the weight of the reasons one has to buy milk from this shop. The request case seems to be different: John creates a reason for Jill by making a request. It seems that the act of request creates a reason for Jill to do as requested. Hiking up the price creates a reason. The reason it creates is ultimately grounded in a further fact, a fact about the customer's well-being. The reason the request creates is ultimately grounded in the request, not in a further fact.

How can requests create reasons for action? The most promising way to explain the reason-giving force of acts of request is this: There are *request norms* like "If and because you are asked to pass the salt you have a reason to do so." How do request norms explain the reason-giving force of requests? Request norms provide answers to the question of whether we should honor particular requests. Consider the following example: Paul asks Kate to pass the salt. Does Kate have a reason to do so? She does, if a request norm of the form "If and because someone asks you to pass the salt, you have a reason to do so" holds. From this, it follows that Kate has a reason to pass the salt. The reasoning is as follows:

1. If and because someone asks you to pass the salt, you have a reason to do so.
2. Paul asks Kate to pass the salt.

Conclusion. Kate has a reason to pass the salt.

Thus, Paul's request to pass the salt creates a reason for Kate to honor the request, provided that this request norm (1) holds. Requests create reasons—and, as we will later see, obligations—if they fall under a request norm.

Why should there be such request norms? There is a norm for honoring such a request if it is valuable for people to follow it (I will return to this point in Chapter 3). A asks B to pass the salt. It is pro tanto good for A to receive the salt, and good to comply with the request because it was made. An act is pro tanto good if its valuable features provide the agent with a reason to perform it. However, doing so may not be good *all things considered*. Consider a case where the requestee has promised a third party not to perform the requested act. Even though the act might be good in itself, it should not be performed, as the promise places the requestee under an obligation *not* to honor the request. Nonetheless, the requested act may still retain its pro tanto goodness. This goodness manifests in various ways: it is good that A gets what she wants, and it is good that A can make her food as spicy as she likes. It is also good to pass the salt because A asked B to do so.

There is a normative structure to request norms: if the requested action is either pro tanto good or not sufficiently bad, the person receiving the request has a reason to honor the request. But why must the act not necessarily be pro tanto good? Why is it enough that the act is simply not sufficiently bad? Consider a case, admittedly hypothetical, where nothing speaks either in favor of or against doing the requested act. In such a scenario, the requestee initially has no independent reason to act. However, the request itself creates a reason to honor the request, and since this reason is not outweighed by any opposing reason, the requestee has a reason to do as requested. Now consider a further case in which a very weak reason speaks against complying. Even then, the request may still provide the requestee with a reason to honor the request, so long as that reason is not outweighed by the weak countervailing consideration. To illustrate this view, consider the following example: A asks B to buy her cigarettes. While supporting A's smoking habit may be bad, it is arguably not as bad as providing reasons that undermine the reason the request itself creates. By contrast, if A asked B to buy her heroin, the reasons against doing so would not be outweighed by the request-dependent reason to honor the request.

Thus, it holds for reasons to honor requests (HR):

> (HR) The requestee has a reason to comply with a request as long as the act requested is *not sufficiently bad* to override the reason created by the request itself.

In addition, the requestee has a reason to honor the request if it is good to do as requested out of respect for the reason-giving authority of the requester. Thus, a norm of responding to requests exists when it is not sufficiently bad to do what the requester wants and good to treat the request as a reason for action. In such cases, the following holds: "If and because A asks B to do x, B has a reason to do x."

A request creates a reason to do as requested if it falls under a request norm. It does fall under a request norm if the requested act is not sufficiently bad and good to do it because the requestee was asked to do as requested. Taking requests as reasons for action in these cases also makes it more likely that a favor is done to someone and will be done out of respect for the requester's reason-giving authority. This is why it is valuable to be able to create this additional reason, and why it is, in general, valuable for us to have the normative power of creating reasons by making requests. The fact that it is valuable for us to have the normative power to create reasons by making requests is the reason why we possess this normative power (see also Schaber 2021).

A favor is something done for someone because it aligns with what that person wants. The action may be good for the requester, but it could also be good for a third party. For example, if you ask your friend to do something kind for your child and she agrees, she is doing *you* a favor by helping *your* child. A favor does not necessarily have to be good for the requester. Someone might ask you to buy her a cigarette, even though she knows she should not smoke. Still, by fulfilling her request, you are doing her a favor, because you are doing what she wants you to do.

The reason created by the request might be overridden by competing reasons. For example, John asks Jill to read his paper. While it would be good for John to receive Jill's feedback and good to do so because he asked, Jill might have other pressing duties that prevent her from fulfilling the request. In this case, the reason created by John's request is defeated by the stronger reasons Jill has to attend to her other obligations. She has a pro tanto reason to read John's paper, but, all things considered, she should not honor his request. If no such overriding reasons exist, the requestee may act as requested. I will return to this point in Chapter 3.

1.7 Do We Need Requests?

The reasons we create by making requests should motivate others to do what we want them to do. However, do we really need requests to achieve this goal?

Weltman doubts whether this is the case because we can motivate others using other means. Weltman writes:

> It's good for me if you can get me to read your draft, because then you owe me, and I can call in that favor later. Often we do this via requests: you request I read the draft, and then later I call in the favor by requesting you read my draft. But we can do this in other ways. We could have a system where you have a box outside your door where you put drafts, and I have a box too, and if I want you to owe me a favor, I can grab a draft out of your box, and if I want to call in the favor, I can call your attention to the draft in my box. It's mysterious what reason-giving force the *request* has, over and above the reason-giving force that the box process has. (Weltman 2022, 5)

Does Weltman's example demonstrate that we do not need requests to get others to do what we want? It does not, as his example is itself an instance of a request. Requests can take various forms—they do not need to be speech acts. Non-verbal communicative acts can also function as requests. The act Weltman refers to is, therefore, a request. By putting the draft in the box, I communicate my desire for you to read it. If I want to give you a reason to read my draft and know that you will interpret my action as a request, I should put the draft in the box. A request can thus be made through nonverbal means, such as placing a draft in a box.

But do we actually need requests to motivate others to do what we want? It is true that I could get you to read my draft by other means than asking you to do so. I could, for instance, offer you money for reading my draft. This would provide you with a reason to do so. Or I could threaten to harm you if you do not read the draft. This would also give you a reason to read my draft.

Thus, why do we need requests? Let us focus on the money offer case. What is the reason for me to ask you to read the draft and not to offer you money for doing so? If I offered you money for reading my draft, you would be reading the draft to get a personal benefit. You would not do it for me. By asking you to do it I offer you the option of doing it for me. This is the relationship I might want to have with you. You do certain things for me, and I do certain things for you. This is what we expect friends or colleagues to do. It would be strang to offer a friend or a colleague money for reading my draft. This is not how friends or colleagues should interact. As a colleague or as a friend you should be willing to do certain things for me. My request to read my draft is thus a reason to do so for a colleague or for a friend, and maybe not for a stranger. And you would not be a colleague or a friend if you did it for money. Requests enable you to act in such situations as a good colleague or a good friend. There are, of course, other ways of getting people to do what you want them to do than offering them money. I can demand that you do what I want you to do. I may manipulate you into doing as I please or force you by threatening you to do as I want. But to change the normative situation by demanding, I need an authority I often do not have. And if I manipulate or force you into doing what I want you to do I wronged you, which I should not and generally do not want to. What makes the power to make requests so valuable is that by requesting something of you, I give you a reason to do what I want you to do that respects your interests and desires. If you honor a request, you do something for someone else.

If you act to avoid a threat or to gain a financial or social reward, you neither treat the requester's desires and interests as reasons, nor do you act out of respect for the other person's reason-giving authority. But you do so if you do something because someone asked you to do it. This is an important aspect of the value that the practice of making and honoring requests holds for us. It allows us to act for one another's sake in a way that no other form of addressing others can achieve.

1.8 Good for Whom?

As mentioned earlier, it is good for all of us to be able to create reasons by requesting. Weltman questions the claim. He writes:

> It is good that requests have reason-giving force: good for who, exactly? It is not obviously good for people who are socially situated such that they are not typically able to issue requests and such that they must accede to many requests, like women in a patriarchal society that forbids them from speaking in various contexts. (Weltman 2022, 6)

The fact that women are not allowed to speak and request things in a patriarchal society is bad and wrong. It is bad and wrong because it is a good thing to have the power to speak and to make requests. This supports the view that having the power to create reasons for others to do what you want them to do is good for all. Therefore, it is bad and wrong if a society prevents some from exercising the power to create reasons for action by making requests.

It would also be bad, Weltman argues, if by making requests we were able to start relationships. He illustrates the point by a society in which it would be terrible if by requesting people were able to form relationships because they are so burdensome.

> Allegedly in Ik society, people found the reciprocity norm so onerous that they went out of their way to avoid situations where they might come to owe someone a favor ... People in a situation like this would say it is terrible that requests can give rise to ... relations . (Weltman 2022, 5n7)

It might well be the case that requests could give rise to relations that are bad for us. But I do not think that this is a problem for the normative view of requests. If a request gives rise to bad relations we should neither make them nor see them as providing us with reasons for action. It is good for us to be able to create reasons by making requests. This does, however, not imply that it is always good to ask others for favors or to be asked by others to do something for them. On the contrary. It might often be bad to be asked to do something. But these requests are not reason-giving and can be turned down or even dismissed. It might not be always easy to turn them down. But we would be justified in doing so. We will return to this point in Chapter 7.

1.9 Summary

The epistemic account of the normativity of requests, which holds that requests have no independent normative force, should be rejected. Requests are not simply informing the requestee of the requester's desire and thereby possibly tracking reasons. When making a request, you communicate the intention to create a reason for the requestee to comply. Requests provide reasons when they align with request norms. They take the form: "If and because A asks B to do x, B has reasons to do x." Request norms provide us with the normative ability to create reasons for others by making requests. Although B might already have independent reasons to do x, A's request adds to these reasons. Requests provide others with the option to perform acts for the other person's sake, for her desires, and out of respect for her reason-giving authority. This is an important aspect of the value the practice of making and honoring requests has for us.

2

Request Norms

2.1 Overview

A asks B to pass the salt. Should B pass A the salt? The answer is 'Yes' if there is a request norm of the form "If and because someone asks you to pass the salt you should pass the salt." The norm tells you that you should pass the salt if and because you were asked to do so. But what are request norms? Are they conventions? Or socially established principles? Or are they norms that obtain regardless of being recognized and part of our social practice? The answers to these questions depend on why these norms apply to us. For instance, why does the request norm "If and because A asks B to pass the salt, B should pass the salt" apply to B?

One might think that B has a reason to honor A's request because it aligns with an accepted norm or because people expect you to honor the request. Alternatively, one might think that the request should be honored because it is the right thing to do. One might also hold the view that a request norm should be followed if and because it is a socially established principle or because it is good that people feel bound to follow the norm.

However, I argue in this chapter that whether a request provides reasons for action depends on the valuable features of the requested act. John asks Jill to read his paper. It would be good for John if Jill, who is familiar with the topic, commented on his paper, and good if she did it because she was asked to do so. I argue that due to these valuable features of the requested act, the request norm exists: "If and because John asks Jill to read his paper, Jill has a reason to read the paper." A request norm exists if it is good or at least not sufficiently bad to do as requested and good to take the request as a reason to act. The latter holds only if the requested act is good or at least not sufficiently bad. A requested act might benefit the requester without being good overall. For example, if A asks B to harm C, this action might benefit A but would not be good. A request creates a reason for action only if doing as requested is not so bad that the reason against doing it outweighs the reason created by the request.

Let us explore these points in greater detail. The chapter has seven parts. The first part distinguishes reasons from obligations. The second part deals with the idea that request norms are conventions we should follow and shows its shortcomings. The third part discusses and criticizes the view that request norms are socially established principles we have reasons to respect. The fourth part deals with Owens's proposal that request norms should be followed if the norm is recognized by a sufficient number of people and good that they feel bound to follow the norm. The fifth part shows how request norms are justified by reference to certain valuable features of honoring the request. The sixth part critically examines the "wishful thinking" objection according to which such norms are the result of an invalid inference from "It is good that p" to "thus p." The seventh part concludes.

2.2 Reasons and Obligations

Request norms can take two forms: (a) "B has a reason to do x if and because B was asked by A to do x," and (b) "B ought to do x if and because B was asked by A to do x." If B ought to do x B has an obligation to act accordingly.

What is meant by having a reason to do x? If B has a reason to pass the salt, there is a consideration speaking in favor of doing so. However, B would not commit a wrong if she did not pass the salt and would thus also not be blameworthy for not doing so. By contrast, if B has an obligation to pass the salt, B would commit a wrong if she flouted the obligation and blame would be warranted. I follow David Owens on this point:

> This is an important difference between being under an obligation to do something for a friend and merely having a reason to do it. I may have a good reason to buy Tim a very nice birthday present. But I'm unlikely to feel *obliged* to do this whilst I do feel obliged to accede to his request for help in

moving house. One difference here is that I won't be blamed for failing to buy him a nice present. (Owens 2012, 99)

You could be blamed for not feeling obliged to help your friend move house and for not doing so. However, you do not warrant blame for failing to buy Tim a nice birthday present.

Thus, the following holds for reasons (R) and obligations (O):

(R) If you have a reason to do *x*, there is something that speaks in favor of doing *x*, but failing to do *x* would not constitute a wrong or warrant blame.

(O) If you are obliged to do *x*, failing to fulfill the obligation constitutes a wrong and warrants blame.

If a request norm applies to you, you have either a reason or an obligation to comply with the request. If someone asks you to pass the salt you have a reason or even an obligation to do so, provided the request norm applies to you. But is this the case? Why should you do what the request norm tells you to do?

There are various answers to this question. Let us look at four answers in turn. One could argue that you should follow the norm (a) if and because others expect you to comply with the request, or (b) if and because it is an established norm, or (c) if and because the norm is valuable and recognized, or finally (d) if and because following the norm is valuable.

2.3 Conventions

The request norm "You should pass the salt if and because you are asked by another person to do so" is, as one might argue, an *accepted norm*. Being an accepted norm can mean different things. In a minimal sense, the term might just refer to the fact that this is what most people do: They pass the salt if they are asked to do so. One might think that you should pass the salt because this is what most others do. You should just follow the common practice.

However, the fact that others follow the mentioned request norm is not a reason to do the same. You should only do what others do if there is a reason to do what others do. The fact that others pass the salt when asked is not a reason for passing the salt yourself. The fact that it is a common practice might have valuable outcomes that provide us with reasons to follow the norm. The fact, however, that others follow the norm does not provide us with a reason to do the same.

Alternatively, one might argue that you should follow request norms because others expect you to honor them. They expect this because they believe it is the right thing to do, and they follow these norms themselves because they think it is what they should do. In this case, the norm can be seen as a *convention*. To be called a "convention," a norm does not have to be followed by everyone. However, if most people believe it is right to comply with a request, the corresponding request norm can be considered a convention.

This is what I refer to as a *conventionalist understanding* of request norms (CR):[1]

> (CR) You should follow a request norm if and because most others consider it the right thing to do and expect you to follow it.

(CR) suggests that you should pass the salt when asked because this is what most people believe you should do. However, this cannot be the reason why you should pass the salt. Why? It could only be a reason to pass the salt if others were correct in thinking that you should do so. Suppose they were wrong in thinking this; then you would have no reason to follow the respective request norm. But if they are right, you should pass the salt if and because you were asked.

The position then becomes this: You should pass the salt if there is a reason to do so, and people are correct in thinking that you should pass it when asked. While this is true, it does not align with the conventionalist interpretation of request norms. Most people might expect you to follow a request norm, but it is not the expectation itself that justifies the norm. Rather, it is the reason you have to pass the salt that does the normative work. Their expectation is reasonable if you indeed have a reason to follow the request norm. The conventionalist interpretation of request norms should therefore be rejected.

2.4 The Principle of Established Practices

Consider a different understanding of request norms, one that draws on Thomas Scanlon's idea of what he calls "the principle of established practices." Scanlon argues that it would be wrong to violate a norm that is generally accepted in a given community simply because it "suits one's convenience" (Scanlon 1998, 339). For instance, it would be wrong if B did not pass the salt after being asked by A to do so, given that it is a widely accepted norm to pass the salt when asked. Scanlon calls this the "Principle of Established Practices":

> What I will call the Principle of Established Practices holds that in situations of this kind, if one of these (nonrejectable) principles is generally (it need not be unanimously) accepted in a given community, then it is wrong to violate it simply because this suits one's convenience. (Scanlon 1998, 339)

Why should we follow an established practice? The practice might be required for the provision of a public good (Owens 2022, 27; Raz 2009, 248). The public good will only be provided if most people do their share in contributing to it. As a member of the relevant community, you should do your share. It would be wrong to flout the relevant norm because it would be unfair. Thus, the reason to follow the norm is provided by a requirement of fairness and—as has to be stressed—not by the fact that it is a widely accepted norm. Honoring requests might also be required by considerations of fairness. Jill asks John to read her paper. She has commented on many of John's papers in the past. It would be unfair of him to turn her request down. However, the request norm "If Jill asks John to read a paper, he has a reason to honor the request" would not hold because it was a widely accepted norm. It would rather hold for reasons of fairness.

Here is another way of reading Scanlon's principle of established practices. Given that a norm is a widely accepted norm is a reason for an agent to follow the norm. Why? Take the salt example again. The fact that the corresponding norm is widely accepted provides the requester A with a reason to expect B to honor her request. The acceptance of the norm leads A to rely on B to pass the salt. A might therefore suffer a slight loss if B did not pass the salt. A would have sat somewhere else if she had known that B would not pass the salt. If B turns down the request A has to walk around the table to get the salt. B has a reason to pass the salt because B should not allow A to suffer a loss. Scanlon writes:

> It can also be wrong to violate the reasonable expectations of others. For example, if in my society members of a family are normally expected to support each other in certain ways then, even if I have not benefited from this practice, it could be wrong for me to allow others to suffer losses as a

result of their expectation that I would follow it. I ought at least to warn them that I cannot be counted on in this way. (Scanlon 1998, 347)

A might suffer a slight loss because A relies on B to pass the salt when asked to do so. A relies on B to pass the salt because A expects B to do so. A could expect B to pass the salt in a *predictive sense*. A could think that B will pass the salt when asked to do so. A could expect B to pass the salt in a *normative sense*. A might think that B ought to pass the salt when asked to do so. To allow A to suffer a slight loss is problematic only if A has a normative expectation that is justified. If A relies on B to pass the salt and B has a reason to do so, to allow someone to suffer a slight loss is wrong. However, it is not wrong if the normative expectation is not justified. The latter holds if B has no reason to pass the salt and the request norm "If and because A asks you to pass the salt, you should pass the salt" does not obtain.

That it would be bad for A if B did not pass the salt might be a reason to follow the request norm in question. However, the fact that A expects B to pass the salt and does therefore rely on B to pass the salt, does as such not provide B with a reason to honor A's request.

A's expectations provide B with a reason only if they are backed by reasons and if A is correct in thinking that B has a reason to pass the salt when asked.

"You should pass the salt if and because asked by someone else to do so" might be the principle of an established practice. The fact that it is a principle of an established practice alone does not provide an agent with a reason for action. If following such a principle had no value, we had no reason to follow it. However, if following an established practice has value, we have reason to follow it. The reason is provided by the *value* the compliance with the established practice has, and not by the fact that it is a principle of an established practice.

2.5 Conventional Obligations

David Owens holds the view that there is a category of norms that are binding because being bound by them is good, and that this can only be the case if the norm is recognized by a sufficient number of people. Owens calls these norms "conventional obligations" (Owens 2022, 70). He writes:

> *Modest Conventionalism*: We are sometimes bound by rule R (where R satisfies *Practice Dependence*) because of the value of being so bound, a deontic value that can necessarily be served only by the recognition of the bindingness of R. (Owens 2022, 70)

What does it mean that a rule or a norm is recognized? On Owens's view, it is not enough that people follow the norm, given that others do. People recognize a norm if they feel obliged to follow it and do so because they believe that it is a good thing to be bound to follow the norm. More precisely, they recognize the norm when they think—as Owens puts it—"(a) that there is positive value in being bound to conform and (b) that others recognize the obligation (in sufficient numbers, etc.) because they too share the same thought" (Owens 2022, 72). Owens argues that recognizing the norm is "valuable for its own sake" (Owens 2022, 72). He states that it is valuable "by bringing us all together in a socially useful enterprise with a deontic structure" (Owens 2022, 72). If we understood request norms as conventional obligations, we would hold the view that people should follow a request norm because it would be good that people felt obliged to do so.

Following the request norm undeniably has instrumental value. For example, it would be beneficial if people felt bound by the salt-passing norm: "If and because someone asks you to pass the salt, you should do so." If the request norm "you should pass the salt if someone asks you to do so" is widely recognized, it is more likely that your request will be honored, and the other person will do what you want them to do. In other words, it increases the likelihood that you will get the salt, which is a desirable outcome. If a request norm is not recognized, it is unlikely to be honored, giving agents fewer reasons to make the request. However, the addressee of an unrecognized request still has reasons to honor the request, provided that honoring the request is valuable. The reason is provided by the valuable features of the requested act. B has a reason to pass the salt, even if the respective request norm is not recognized by B, the requestee.

B has a reason to pass the salt if something is speaking in favor of B doing so. The fact that the request norm is recognized is not a reason to follow the norm. It is rather a reason for A to ask B to pass the salt. A's request would have created a reason even if the norm was not recognized, because it is good to honor the request regardless of its being recognized. However, A has more reason to ask B to pass the salt if B is likely to honor the request. If the norm of honoring requests is not recognized, it is unlikely that A's request would be fulfilled by B or anyone else. The recognition of request norms provides agents with reasons to make requests, rather than reasons to honor them.

2.6 Request Norms and Valuable Features

When does the request norm "If and because A asks B to pass the salt, B has a reason to pass the salt" exist? I think it exists if and because the following two conditions are met: (a) it is good or at least not sufficiently bad to pass the salt and (b) it is good to take A's request to pass the salt as a reason to do so. It is good to take A's request as a reason if it is good to do as requested out of respect for A's reason-giving authority. This holds only if what A wants B to do is itself not sufficiently bad. An action is not sufficiently bad if its bad-making properties do not provide the requestee with decisive reasons not to do it. The reason a requestee may have for not doing something that would be pro tanto bad can be outweighed by the reason created by the request itself. In such cases, the requestee has reason to honor the request, even if doing so is not pro tanto good.

However, it is not always good to take a request as a reason for action and act out of respect for the reason-giving authority of the requester. Sometimes, doing so can be wrong. For instance, it is wrong to treat a request as a reason if the requested act would be disrespectful to third parties. By contrast, it is good to treat a request as a reason for action when it would be good to honor the request out of respect for the requester's reason-giving authority. In some cases, it may be wrong to treat a request as a reason, namely, when the requested action should not be performed merely because it was requested. Consider the following example: Jill wants to leave her partner Jeff, but Jeff asks her to stay. Jill should not remain with him simply because he asked her to. If she does stay, it should be for independent reasons, such as love. In such cases, it would be wrong to act out of respect for Jeff's reason-giving authority because a request is not the right reason to continue an intimate relationship with another person.

Whether a request provides reasons for action depends on the valuable features of honoring the request. However, it remains uncertain whether all valuable features necessarily provide reasons for action. For instance, it might be good for A if B were to do x. One perspective suggests that everyone capable of doing x has a reason to do so, regardless of their relationship with A. Alternatively, another perspective argues that only those who share a specific relationship with A, such as friends, have a reason to do x.

Regardless of which perspective is correct, reasons to adhere to a request norm stem from the valuable features of honoring the request. For example, a request norm like "If and because A asks B to pass the salt, B should pass the salt" applies to B only if passing the salt is good or at least not sufficiently bad, and good to take it as a reason. It would not be good to take it as a reason if passing the salt was sufficiently bad.

2.7 P Is Good, Therefore p

The argument is that a request norm of the form "If and because A asks B to do x, B has a reason to do x" obtains only if it is good that B follows the norm. Is this an invalid inference from "x is good, therefore x exists" ("it is good that people follow the request norm x, therefore the request norm x obtains")? This is what is sometimes called "the wishful thinking" objection. The issue was raised by Enoch. He writes:

> Perhaps it would be nice if there were moral luck. How is this any reason to believe that there is moral luck? Thus stated, such inferences look ridiculous, paradigmatic cases of wishful thinking. (Enoch 2009, 222)

Enoch argues that in some cases the inference might be valid.

> Such arguments can be neither accepted nor rejected en bloc. Rather, what the proponent of such an argument owes us to vindicate her (suspicious) argument. (Enoch 2009, 224)

Enoch is not sure what vindicating such an argument looks like. However, it might hold, he thinks, for moral cases (see also Sayre-McCord 2024). He writes:

> It is not a generally valid inferential rule, but for some operators—and perhaps especially moral ones—it may very well be. (Enoch 2009, 224)

Is it a valid inference to conclude that a request norm exists if and because it is good that people follow the norm? The question regarding request norms is whether the given value-based explanation of request norms shows why these norms apply to us. Consider again the salt example. It is good that B passes the salt. It is good that B takes A's request as a reason to comply with A's request. This is what provides B with reasons to follow the respective request norm ("B has a reason to pass the salt if A asks you to do so"). What is assumed here is that reasons for action can be explained by reference to valuable features of the acts concerned. It is not assumed that all reasons can be explained by valuable features.[2] There might be reasons for action that are not based on valuable features of acts. But if some reasons are based on valuable features of acts, the norm that tells us to act in a certain way can be explained by the values the norm serves (see also Bruno 2022, 3221).[3] And so does the value of getting the salt and of taking the request as a reason explain the existence of the respective request norm. It explains the existence of the request norm by explaining what it is that provides us with reasons to follow the request norm and do what is requested.

Sometimes, it is good, or at least not sufficiently bad, to perform a requested act and do so because one was asked. If this is the case, a request norm obtains. The request norm provides the agent the norm applies to with the normative ability to create additional reasons by making requests. If the request norm "If and because A asks B to do x, B has reasons to do x" obtains A has the normative ability to create reasons by requesting B to do x. It is good to be able to create reasons if doing x is pro tanto good or not sufficiently bad and good to do it out of respect for the reason-giving authority of the requester. Thus, it is good for us to have the normative power to create reasons in such situations. To be able to create reasons makes it more likely that a request is honored and something good is done. It is not an invalid inference from "it is good to do as requested" to the norm "there is a reason to do as requested." If you do not reject the idea that there is a connection between what is good and what we have reasons to do, the inference in question is not a form of wishful thinking.

The skeptic might still question whether such request norms truly exist. However, request norms exist when there are reasons to follow them. Are there such reasons? I argue that the valuable features of the acts in question provide us with these reasons. It is their value that speaks in favor of performing them. Raz writes:

> The good of what is of value determines for what conduct if provides reason, understanding the value depends on and leads to understanding the reason … If the connection between the value of something and the action for which it is a reason is not arbitrary (and it cannot be arbitrary) then it must be determined by the value. That is, the value of something to be a reason for an action it must determine what the action is, and it must be an essential property or aspect of what makes the valuable things valuable, which determines the action. (Raz 2001, 165)

2.8 Summary

The normative force of requests can be explained by drawing on request norms. Request norms have the form "If and because A asks B to do x, B should do x." There is a request norm "If and because A asks B to do x, B should do x" if and because it is good or not sufficiently bad for A that B does x, and good that B does it because she was asked. B's reason for doing x is not provided by the fact that others expect B to do so. B's reason is also not provided by the fact that most people think it is the right thing to do, or that it is good that B feels bound to do it. The reason B has to do x is provided by the goodness or the insufficient badness of doing x and the additional goodness of doing x because asked.

It is valuable that request norms are recognized. Their recognition makes it more likely that people act for the reasons that are created by requests. The recognition of request norms makes it thus more likely that people do things that are good like passing the salt and reading other people's drafts. However, a request norm exists independently of its being recognized. The request norm

"If and because A asks B to pass the salt, B should pass the salt" exists because following this norm has valuable features. If B recognizes the request norm in question, B is more likely to honor the request, thereby doing others a favor and something good by respecting the requester's reason-giving authority. If B recognizes the request norm, she recognizes the reasons she has to honor A's request.

3

The Obligation and Reason Creating Force of Requests

The preceding chapters argued that requests sometimes create reasons and sometimes obligations. The view that requests create reasons has been criticized. Yotam Benziman, David Cupit, and Micha Gläser argue instead that requests create obligations (Benziman 2023; Cupit 1994; Gläser 2019). Should we agree? I argue that requests sometimes create reasons and sometimes obligations.

3.1 Overview

In this chapter, I will explore when requests create reasons for action and when they create obligations. I argue that a request creates a reason for the requestee if, and only if, it is good to treat the request as a reason for action. This is possible only if the requested action is good or not sufficiently bad. However, even if it is good to take the request as a reason, the requestee may have reasons to turn the request down. The requestee is permitted to honor the request if the reason created by the request is not defeated by any conflicting reasons. If the request-dependent reason is defeated by conflicting reasons, the requestee is rationally or morally not permitted to honor the request.

I also argue that requests can also create reasons for future actions. They create reasons that will apply to the requestee at a later time, provided that the request-independent reasons for doing the requester a favor still exist. The request-dependent reasons for future actions can be removed by revoking the earlier request. The requester may revoke the earlier request if she is competent to do so—that is, if she is capable of making reasoned decisions when she revokes her earlier request.

In other cases, requests can create obligations. Whether a request creates an obligation depends on the normative structure of the relationship between the requester and the requestee. Consider this: you have certain obligations toward a friend. You are obliged to do important things for your friend if she asks you to. For instance, you have an obligation to help your friend if she asks you to. Thus, if your friend requests your assistance in moving house, her request imposes an obligation on you. Crucially, this obligation arises specifically because of her request; without it, you would not be required to help her move house.

In contrast, some obligations exist independently of requests. For example, if your friend asks you not to harm her, the obligation not to harm her is not created by her request; it exists regardless of whether you have been asked not to harm her. You are obliged not to harm anyone, including her, regardless of whether she explicitly requests it. By comparison, helping your friend move house is contingent on her request and the nature of your relationship.

I also argue that whether requests create reasons or obligations depends on the normative structure of the relationship between requester and requestee, that is, on what we owe each other as friends, colleagues, or strangers. If a stranger asks you to help move house, you are not obliged to comply, though you might have a reason to assist. If your friend asks you to help her move house, you are arguably obliged to honor her request.

As mentioned above, you can honor a request for both request-dependent and request-independent reasons. But should you honor requests simply because you were asked?

I argue that while you cannot choose the reasons that motivate your actions, acting on request-dependent reasons can add particular value to the act. Helping your friend because she requested it is better than helping her only for request-independent reasons. However, while it is good to act on request-dependent reasons, you cannot be obliged to do so because you cannot choose the reasons you act on. In summary, requests may create reasons for action or, in certain contexts, obligations. This distinction depends on the normative structure of the relationship between the requester and the requestee.

Let us examine these points in greater detail. This chapter is structured as follows: The first part critically examines Cupit's view that requests create obligations. The second part discusses Gläser's proposal that requests create prima facie obligations rather than reasons, as well as Benziman's idea that they create imperfect obligations, and it highlights the difficulties both proposals face. The third part discusses James Lewis's account of the normativity of requests and explains why it should be rejected. The fourth part discusses the idea that requests only create reasons within personal relationships and argues that the reason-giving force of requests does not presuppose the existence of a personal relationship. The fifth part explores the role relationships play in altering the normative landscape by sometimes creating reasons and sometimes creating obligations. The sixth part compares the proposed account of the normative force of requests with Enoch's account. The seventh part addresses how requests for future favors create reasons for action. The eighth part addresses the strength of request-dependent reasons, arguing that they vary depending on the relationship between the requester and the requestee. The ninth part explores whether requests create additional reasons for actions we are already obligated to perform, concluding that they do not. The tenth part considers whether we should comply with requests for request-dependent reasons, arguing that while we cannot choose which reasons to act on, it is nonetheless good to comply simply because one was asked. The eleventh and final part concludes the chapter.

3.2 Do Requests Create Obligations?

Geoffrey Cupit argues that, under ordinary circumstances, requests create obligations. They do not create obligations only if (a) the requestee is asked to do something wrong (Cupit 1994, 453) or (b) the request treats the requestee as subservient (Cupit 1994, 454). Cupit believes that in all other cases, requests create obligations.

Here is Cupit's argument: The requestee makes a fool of the requester if she turns down the request, provided that "the requestor trusts the requestee to ·e the request as providing a reason for action. In the absence of trust, there is no (unwarranted) belief for the requestee to act upon" (Cupit 1994, 453). According to Cupit, this trust is what a requester typically demonstrates: they trust the requestee to treat their request as a reason for action. A requester believes that the requestee is a person "for whom our wishes, in themselves, can provide a reason for action. To request is to treat the requestee as such a person, as someone who is not cold, uncaring, indifferent, unloving, or disregardful" (Cupit 1994, 450). Thus, if the requestee rejects the request, the requester is made to look foolish. Since we are obliged not to treat others as fools, we are therefore obliged to honor their requests. Cupit writes:

> Why should it be inappropriate to speak of an obligation arising in the case of a request? Certainly, the requirement that there be a "previous committing action" is satisfied. Further, this reason for action generated by requests is grounded in the duty not to degrade and thus wrong the requester. (Cupit 1994, 454)

According to this view, requesters who trust the requestee to honor their requests are wronged if their requests are turned down.

Should we agree with this? There are several difficulties with Cupit's proposal. First, it is unclear whether requesters, in ordinary circumstances, truly trust the requestee to honor their requests. Often, they may only hope that their requests will be fulfilled.[1] The requester might not trust the requestee to treat the request as a reason for action but still try to persuade them to honor the request.

Second, when the requester does trust the requestee to honor the request, she relies on the requestee to fulfill the request. If the requestee declines, the requester may feel let down. However, this reliance may not always be warranted. Reliance would be justified if the requestee had, for example, promised to honor the request. In such a case, the requestee would be under an obligation to fulfill the request, but this obligation is created by the promise, not by the request. If the reliance is unwarranted, the requestee is not obliged to honor the request. The requester may feel disappointed if the request is refused, but they are not made a fool by the requestee turning it down.

The requestee may still be obliged to honor the request, but not for the reasons Cupit suggests. A requestee is not obliged to honor the request because of a general obligation not to make fools of others. Instead, the obligation might arise from some other obligation the requestee has toward the requester, triggered by the request. We will return to this point later in the chapter.

Cupit may have something else in mind. His idea might be that requests create obligations to treat the request "as providing a reason for action" (Cupit 1994, 450). In this view, a request does not create an obligation to honor the request but rather an obligation to consider the request as a reason for action. The request must be seen as something that counts in favor of honoring it, even if other reasons might weigh against it. The requestee makes a fool of the requester only if they refuse to take the request as a reason for action. Is this the obligation that is created by requests?

I do not think so for the following reason. The requestee does not wrong the requester by disregarding the request if honoring it would be wrong. Failing to consider a request constitutes a wrong only if the request creates a reason for action. We will return to this point in section 3.6.

3.3 Prima Facie and Imperfect Obligations

a. Prima Facie Obligations

On Micha Gläser's view, requests do not create reasons but rather "prima facie obligations" (Gläser 2019, 44). He rejects what he calls the "mere addition account" of requests (Gläser 2019, 31), according to which requests add further reasons to those already supporting the requested act. If A asks B to do x, B is, on his view, obliged to do x, even though not under a strict obligation. That means that B may turn down the request but is still obliged to consider the ends A is pursuing through the request. Gläser argues that this account is preferable to the "mere addition account" because the latter struggles to explain situations where the requester is wronged by the rejection of their request and can therefore justifiably complain. He illustrates this with the following example:

> *Movie Night*
>
> Rick and Erica are friends. They live across town from each other. Erica is very good with computers, while Rick is not. Rick has a critical deadline the

> next day at noon but is having trouble with his laptop. After attempting to fix it himself with no success, he reaches out to Erica, asking her to come over tonight to help. She responds that, while she feels for him, she'd rather stay in and watch a movie. (Gläser 2019, 33)

Gläser argues that the resentment Rick feels in this situation is a proper response to how Erica treated his request. It is appropriate because "she, in some way, wronged him" (Gläser 2019, 34). He adds: "Yet this is precisely what the mere addition account seems to deny" (Gläser 2019, 34). According to Gläser, requests like Rick's do not create additional reasons but "prima facie obligations." It is not necessarily the case that one is under a strict obligation to honor a request like Rick's. However, Gläser argues that requests play a key role in a joint enterprise aimed at harmonizing ends. Requests do not impose strict obligations but often leave it to the requestee to decide whether or not to honor the request. They are framed with speech acts like "feel free not to do it" (Gläser 2019, 44). Requestees are free to refuse requests but are nonetheless obliged to consider the ends that the request is meant to achieve.

Gläser illustrates this further with Erica turning down Rick's request for babysitting:

> Note here how natural it would be for her to respond with a counter-proposal along the lines of: "I can't tonight, but how about I come over first thing in the morning?" She would thereby be expressing her bonafide cooperation in constructing a reasonable harmony of ends between them. (Gläser 2019, 46)

The idea here is that Erica might turn down the request, but she is still obliged to signal her willingness to address the ends involved.

Gläser is right in suggesting that requests do not merely create additional reasons for action. Sometimes, they create obligations. *Movie Night* seems to be such a case, Erica wrongs Rick by refusing to help and gives him a reason to complain. However, there are clear cases where the mere addition account is more fitting than Gläser's "prima facie obligation" account. Consider this case: I ask a colleague whom I have never met to review my draft because she is an expert in the field. She turns down my request, saying that she has no time to read because of the manuscript she has to submit soon. In this scenario, she has not wronged me, and I have no reason to complain. While it might be kind of her to read my draft, she has neither an obligation to do so nor any obligation to take care of the philosophical goals I am pursuing.

Erica may owe Rick an alternative when refusing his request because they are friends and he needs help. However, she would not be under an obligation to offer an alternative if a stranger asked her to babysit, neither a strict nor a prima facie obligation. A stranger's request does not create an obligation, as we do not have the far-reaching obligations of cooperation that Gläser assumes. Erica would not wrong a stranger by refusing such a request, nor would the stranger have any legitimate reason to complain. Why? Because we do not owe strangers this kind of assistance.

b. Imperfect Obligations

Yotam Benziman argues that requests place the requestees under "imperfect" obligations (Benziman 2023). The thought is this: a request is made because the requester needs what she is asking for. Benziman writes:

> (The requester) initiates it because she needs it, and thus she exposes … her vulnerability. Refusing to grant the favor would therefore be … rude, inconsiderate, and even morally wrong. (Benziman 2023, 302)

Requests create on this account obligations. As Benziman argues, it is morally wrong not to honor them, "precisely because the favor has been requested" (Benziman 2023, 298). However, they do not create perfect obligations that have to be fulfilled "no matter what" (Benziman 2023, 302). They allow the requestee discretion and leave it up to the requestee to honor the request. We ask for favors, we do not demand favors (see Benziman 2023, 302). Benziman comcludes that requests create *imperfect obligations.* Perfect obligations must be fulfilled "no matter what" (Benziman 2023, 302), whereas imperfect obligations "leave us the discretion to decide when, where, and how to fulfill them" (Benziman 2023, 302).

Do requests create imperfect obligations? Benziman's proposal faces several difficulties. (a) It is unclear what it means to have an imperfect obligation. Consider a case where A asks B to pass the salt. If this request creates an imperfect obligation, B may refuse. Passing the salt would not be something

B is required to do; otherwise, B would be under a perfect obligation to do so. Thus, refusing the request would not necessarily be morally wrong. If declining were morally wrong, B would, by definition, be under a perfect obligation to comply.

Benziman might argue that refusing the request is only wrong if B consistently refuses requests to pass the salt, but it is not morally wrong in a single, particular instance.

If it is not morally wrong to refuse to pass the salt in a particular case, then it is permissible to turn down the request. Thus, B is not obliged to pass the salt but merely has a reason to do so. This reasoning appears to apply to all particular cases where someone has been asked to pass the salt, making the concept of an imperfect obligation difficult to understand. If it is understood as a reason to comply it is not understood as an obligation. If it is understood as an obligation it is not understood as something that may be turned down.

(b) Benziman argues that the requestee should honor a request because the requester needs it. However, the phrase "needs it" is ambiguous and requires further clarification. It must signify more than simply wanting something to happen. In this context, it could mean that failing to meet the needs of others causes them significant distress. Benziman argues that "seeing another in their distress is a strong reason for helping them" (2023, 303).

This may well be true. However, not all requests reveal genuine needs. Many requests simply express desires that are not of critical importance to the requester. Consider the case where someone says, "If you have time to read my paper, that would be nice. But it would not be a problem if you did not have time." If the desire expressed by the request is not fulfilled, it would not result in a significant loss. Similarly, if A asks B to pass the salt at the dinner table and B does not do as requested, C might step in and fulfill the request instead. In such a case, B's refusal to honor the request would result in no loss at all. In this situation, A might remark, "It would have been nice if B had passed me the salt, but now C has done it, and I got what I wanted." Since nothing serious is at stake for A in this scenario, it is reasonable to conclude that B was not obliged to pass the salt; rather, B simply had a reason to do so.

3.4 Lewis's Account

Various authors argue that requests are only reason-giving if a certain relationship between requester and requestee obtains. James Lewis, for instance, holds the view that a requestee has a reason to do as requested if and only if the requestee "places sufficient discretionary value" (Lewis 2018, 12) in the person who asked her to do (or omit) something. The discretionary value is understood as a value the requestee is not obliged to place in the requester: "These are attitudes that one is not obliged to hold" (Lewis 2018, 12). If the requester does not put value in the requester she does not have a reason to do as requested. The request creates a reason by way of the requestee placing value in the requester.

On this view, John's asking Jill to read his draft provides Jill with a reason if and only if Jill places sufficient discretionary value in John. Lewis thinks that this proposal can account for the discretionary quality of requests. It is up to the requestee to decide whether she honors the request. This is how requests differ from orders. Orders are attempts to put others under an obligation, requests attempt to provide others with a reason. Lewis thinks that his account of the reason-giving force of request can explain why this is the case (Lewis 2018, 14): Requests have a discretionary quality because they are based on valuing-attitudes toward the requester the requestee is not obliged to have. Lewis writes:

> One intends for the other to treat this request as a reason, but not for them to treat it as itself conclusively instructing them. We ask them to Φ, and thereby acknowledging that whilst our wishes are clear, the matter of whether to Φ or not is up to them. (Lewis 2018, 11)

A request gives the requestee a reason if and only if the requestee holds certain valuing attitudes toward the requester. It is up to the requestee to acquire these attitudes. On this account, it is not up to the requester to create a reason for the requestee. Lewis argues that when we make requests we sometimes "implicitly appeal to the addresses to value us" (Lewis 2018, 13)—appeals that might sometimes be successful. John might indicate that he is desperate and hopes that this prompts Jill to feel pity for him. If he is successful Jill has a reason, if this is not the case Jill has no reason to do as requested. The reason-giving force of requests is on this account not limited to requests of people the requestees already know.

Lewis cites the case of two strangers, Carrie and Anita. Carrie is looking for a place to hide and knocks on Anita's door asking her whether she can come in without explaining why (Lewis 2018, 13). Carrie appeals to Anita "to take up some valuing-attitude" (Lewis 2018, 13) and might well be successful in doing so. The value-attitude might be "admiration, affection, pity, some kind of endearment" (Lewis 2018, 13). If Anita takes up one of these attitudes, Carrie's request is a reason for Anita to let her in. Lewis thinks that it is a "central merit of the account that I am proposing is its capacity to explain the sense in which the reasons presented in requests are discretionary" (Lewis 2018, 14). He understands discretionary reasons as nonobligatory reasons. Requests provide addressees with reasons for action because they are based on value-attitudes of the requesters they are not obliged to have.

Lewis's proposal faces the following difficulty. It is not clear whether Lewis's account is—as he claims—able to account for the discretionary quality of requests. On his view, Anita has only a reason to let Carrie in if Anita feels, for instance, pity for Carrie. This would be a case of having a certain value-attitude toward Carrie. Anita places discretionary value in Carrie by feeling pity for her. Her valuing provides her with a reason to let Carrie in. The proposal is based on the view that "valuing X is having a favorable attitude towards X such that X can be the source of reasons for action" (Lewis 2018, 6).[2]

The proposal faces difficulties if an alternative view is correct, according to which valuing attitudes provide us with reasons only if they are appropriate. It might not be appropriate for Anita to feel pity for Carrie. The value she places in Carrie would then not be the value she should place in her. Whether it is appropriate would depend on Carrie's situation and would thus not be at Anita's discretion. The discretionary quality of requests could not be traced back to the valuing-attitudes the requestees have no reason to hold. If this was the case, Lewis's model would not explain the normative force of requests.

One could argue that Lewis might counter this objection by amending his account. On an amended account, two things are required for a request to be reason-giving: (a) the requestee has to place value in the requester and

(b) doing so has to be appropriate. The problem is that this account does not fit with Lewis's view of the discretionary quality of requests. On his view, their reason-giving force is entirely up to the requestee. However, on the amended account, it would only be partly up to the requestee. That's because, while (a) is up to the requestee, (b) is not. So the reason-giving force of a request would only be up to the requestee if placing value in the requester was appropriate. Then the force of the request would be up to the requestee's valuing the requester. In all other cases, the reason-giving force of the request would not be up to the requestee. If the requestee places value in the requester but doing so is not appropriate, the request would not be reason-giving.

Of course, Lewis's view of valuing might be correct. It is, however, not obvious that it is and thus not obvious that he can account for the normative force of requests. The account is unacceptable to those who believe that valuing attitudes provide reasons only if they are appropriate.

More importantly, the discretionary normativity of requests can be accounted for without appealing to the valuing attitudes of the requestee. It would be good for Carrie to hide. The reasons created by requests do not necessarily put the requestees under an obligation to honor the request. Anita has a reason to let Carrie in. The reasons she has to do so might leave it at Anita's discretion to honor or not honor Carrie's request. They would leave it to her discretion if the reasons she had for letting her in were not weightier than the reasons against it. We will get back to this in Chapter 7.

3.5 Special Relationships

According to another view, requests create reasons only if the requester and the requestee share a personal relationship. For example, if my partner asks me to do something, I have a reason to honor her request. The same arguably applies to requests from friends, family members, and possibly colleagues. In the case of Jill and John, who are colleagues, John's request gives Jill a reason to read his draft.

By contrast, consider asking a stranger for directions to the train station. Since you and the stranger lack a special relationship, your request, according to this view, does not create an additional reason for her to honor the request. She might have a request-independent reason to help, such as the fact that you are lost and need directions, but your request itself would not provide a new reason. In this case, your request merely informs her of a reason that already exists—its role is epistemic, not normative. Thus, your request to the stranger for directions does no normative work; it merely makes the request-independent reason visible.

Dan Khokhar defends what he calls the "relational view" of requests, which holds that "requests are an important tool for conducting our interpersonal relationships" (Khokhar 2022, 11). Why does he believe this to be the case? Let us take a closer look at Khokhar's understanding of the reason-giving force of requests. Requests allow us to decide which interests of others are important to us. Additionally, they serve the need for recognition in intimate relationships. Khokhar writes:

> Now when you do something for me because I ask you to, you implicitly recognize the significance of my autonomy interest in determining the obligations you owe to me as a friend. One can be moved by a pet's need for food, but that's quite different from being moved by your friend asking for help. The latter involves being seen as someone who can autonomously contribute to the structure of the relationship, and that form of recognition is itself something we have reason to care about. (Khokhar 2022, 11)

When you do something for me because I asked you, you recognize me as someone whose interests have special importance due to our relationship. For Khokhar, it is valuable for a requester to be able to create reasons—or even impose obligations—on the requestee "within the context of an intimate relationship" (Khokhar 2022, 11). For example, if your friend asks you to help her move house, she provides you with a reason, and possibly even with an obligation, to honor the request. You should do it because she asked, and in doing so, you acknowledge her as a friend.

In contrast, if your neighbor asks for help moving house, the relational view suggests that the request itself would not create a reason for you to help. It would be good if you helped your neighbor simply because she needs assistance, not because she asked. The neighbor's request would neither create a reason to help nor impose any obligation on you because you lack the necessary relationship for requests to have a reason or obligation creating force.

Requests provide people with whom we have a special relationship with reasons for action, and sometimes even obligations. But what about a stranger asking you for directions to the station? Does the stranger's request not provide you with a reason to do as requested? Khokhar expresses ambivalence on this issue. As he puts it, he is "of two minds about this question. On the one hand, we might accept that we have an autonomy interest in determining the moral obligations that strangers owe to us simply as fellow persons" (Khokhar 2022, 13). However, he adds:

> On the other hand, I'm also tempted to claim that the power to request plays a distinctive role within interpersonal relationships (and intimate ones in particular). In part, I'm far less certain that the autonomy interest I have in determining the obligations my friends owe to me has a parallel in the case of strangers. (Khokhar 2022, 13)

Following this reasoning, requests made by strangers might not themselves create reasons for action, but instead serve as speech acts that track existing, request-independent reasons the stranger may already have to fulfill the request. Khokhar illustrates this with an example:

> Suppose I ask you for directions to the Louvre because I'm hopelessly lost in Paris. If you tell me how to get there simply to impress your date with your cultural knowledge, I don't think I'd be that bothered. (Khokhar 2022, 13)

However, if a friend did the same simply to impress others, rather than because you asked for help, you might be bothered. This is because, according to the relational view, "requests between intimates function in importantly different ways from requests between strangers" (Khokhar 2022, 14).

Do requests only create reasons for action for requestees with whom we have a special relationship? Khokhar argues that we have an autonomy interest in determining what friends, colleagues, and others we are close to owe us. But as he concedes, we may also have an autonomy interest in shaping normative relations with strangers. Requests might help shape these normative relations not just with friends and partners but with all fellow humans. While requests between intimates may indeed function differently from those between strangers, it would still be good if you helped a stranger. For instance, telling the stranger how to get to the station because they asked would be good, and it would be good to do it because she asked. Even if the stranger would not mind that you did it to impress someone, it would have been better if you did it out of genuine concern for her. And because it would have been good to tell her how to get to the station—and good to do so because she asked—her request provided you with a reason to help her.

3.6 Creating Reasons and Obligations

Requests sometimes create reasons for action, and sometimes they create obligations. But when do they create reasons, and when do they create obligations? Suppose A asks B to do x. There may be different types of request-independent reasons for B to do x. B might have a reason to do x because (a) it is good for B, (b) it is good for third parties, or (c) it is good for A. For example, it might be good for you to read a paper that your colleague asked you to read (a). Honoring your partner's request to look after the children tonight might be good for the children (b). Receiving insightful comments on your paper from your colleague might be good for you (c).

When does a request create a reason for action? Let me return to the discussion from the previous chapters. In Chapter 1, I argued that a request should be honored if the requested act is good or at least not sufficiently bad and if it is good to treat the request as a reason for action. Consider John's request that Jill read his paper. John's request gives Jill a reason to do so: it is good to read the paper, and it is also good to read it because John asked, namely, out of respect for his reason-giving authority. However, taking a request as a reason for action is not always good. It is not good to do so when the requested act is sufficiently bad and the reason created by the request is not strong enough to outweigh the reason not to do as requested. Then the respective request should not be honored. Similarly, a request should not be made if the requested act should not be performed because it was requested. Brenda wants to leave her partner, Jeff. Jeff wants her to stay and asks her to stay ("please do not leave";

It might be good for Jeff if Brenda stayed with him. However, his request is not a reason for her to stay. If she stays, she should stay for other reasons. It would thus not be good to take Jeff's request as a reason to do as requested. His request does, therefore, not create a reason to honor his request.

From these considerations, we can derive a general principle about the reason-giving force of requests (RGR):

> (RGR): A's request creates a reason for B to do as requested if the requested act is good or at least not sufficiently bad and good to take A's request as a reason for action.

John's request may create a reason for Jill to read his draft. However, the reason might be defeated by conflicting reasons. Jill is overwhelmed with work: she needs to finish her manuscript and take care of her children. If these reasons defeat the ones created by John's request, Jill should not honor John's request. She has, in this case, a pro tanto reason to honor and a stronger reason not to honor the request.

Thus, whether one may or should honor a request depends on the balance of reasons that applies to the requestee. Let me clarify what I take this balance of reasons to involve.[3]

Suppose B asks A to do x. A may have reasons to do x, and simultaneously, reasons not to do x. One might hold that if the reasons against are stronger, then A should not do x. In such a case, refraining from x would be the rationally or morally required action.

On my view, A should do x only if there is a decisive reason to do so. Conversely, A should not do x only if there is a decisive reason not to. In many instances, the balance of reasons may leave the decision open. A may permissibly choose whether or not to do x. This can occur when the reasons involved are incommensurable or simply not decisive.

Consider the following case: B asks A to read her paper. A is busy working on her own manuscript, which gives her some reason to decline the request. However, these reasons may not amount to a decisive reason *not* to read B's paper. Now, contrast that with another case: A has promised C to help her move. If keeping this promise is incompatible with reading B's paper, then A has a decisive reason to decline B's request. The promise creates an obligation, and that obligation gives A a decisive reason to help C rather than honor B's request.

This leads to a further principle about the reason-giving force of requests (RGR*):

> *(RGR):** B may do what A asks her to do if and only if the reason created by A's request is not defeated by a decisive reason against doing so.

If B may honor A's request, B does not commit a wrong if B turns the request down and cannot be blamed for doing so. B can only be blamed for turning down the request if B is obliged to do x.

Whether B is obliged to do x depends on what B owes to A. As a friend, B might be obliged to do x when asked by A, while as a colleague, B might have a reason to do x when A asks. It is the normative structure of the relationship between the requester and the requestee that determines whether requests create reasons or obligations. A request creates an obligation by specifying a general background obligation the requester has toward the requestee. I have a general obligation to care for my children. I owe it to both my children and my partner to do my share. My partner's request for me to look after the children tonight creates an obligation by specifying this general obligation.

The corresponding request norm (TCC) can be expressed as follows:

> (TCC) If your partner asks you to look after the children, you are under an obligation to do so, unless you have a decisive reason against doing so.

My partner's request should not be taken merely as a reason to look after the children. Against the background of a general obligation to do my share in caring for our children, my partner's request imposes an obligation on me to do so. The normative force of requests—whether they create reasons or obligations—depends on what we owe as requestees to the requester. I have a general obligation to participate in the care of our children, but I do not have a general obligation to read a draft of a colleague I have never met. Unlike the request of a colleague I have never met to read his paper, my partner's request to look after the children tonight specifies a general obligation.

Thus, it holds for obligation-creating requests (OCR):

> (OCR) A's request that B does x creates an obligation for B to do x if and only if A's request specifies a general obligation B has toward A.

When requests create obligations, they do so not because the requester intends to impose an obligation on the requestee. For example, my partner communicates her intention to give me a reason to look after the children; she does not intend to impose an obligation on me. If she intended the latter, she would be ordering me rather than asking. Her request adheres to a request norm that establishes the obligation: "You should look after the children if your partner asks you to." While she does not want to impose an obligation, she is, nonetheless, creating an obligation by specifying the general obligation I have in caring for our children. Requests create reasons or obligations depending on what we owe each other as strangers, neighbors, colleagues, relatives, friends, and partners.

This leads to two principles regarding the obligation-creating (OCR) and reason-creating (RCR) force of requests:

> (OCR) A request creates an obligation to comply if and only if it specifies a general obligation the requestee already has toward the requester.
>
> (RCR) A request creates a reason if and because it is good or at least not sufficiently bad to do as requested and good to take the request as a reason.

It is important to note here that you may do something good for another person without having been asked by her to do so. For example, if you see that I am looking for salt, you may pass it to me without being asked, acting on the reason my desire provides. In this case, you are acting in my interest, but not specifically because I requested it. Conversely, if I had asked you for the salt, your action would have been directly linked to my request, and the request is arguably a reason for you to pass me the salt.

You may act on purely request-independent reasons if the act does not require consent; you may not if it does. Consider a case where I leave my manuscript on a table after discussing it with you. Even if I would be pleased if you read and commented on it, you would not be permitted to take it without my consent, as taking and reading my draft requires my permission. You would have an obligation not to take my manuscript without my consent. This obligation is a consent-sensitive one (see also Tadros 2016, 204): "You ought not to take my manuscript unless I consent." If you took my manuscript without my consent, you would wrong me. For consent-requiring acts, you are prohibited from acting on reasons that are independent of the request. For example, you might have a reason, unrelated to any request, to read my manuscript, but you are not permitted to take and read it without my consent. I might not want you to read it, and in that case, doing so without my permission would be impermissible. However, if I do want you to read it, I may ask you to do so. In explicitly requesting that you read my manuscript, I thereby grant you permission to take and read it. My request implicitly includes my consent to your taking the manuscript (we have discussed this issue at length in Chapter 1). After all, it would make no sense for me to try to provide you with a reason to read my manuscript if I considered your reading of it to be impermissible.

As discussed in Chapter 1, Weltman argues that a request "alters the normative situation, because my request constitutes consent, and consent modifies the situation" (Weltman 2023, 17). Certain requests indeed provide evidence that the requester consents to the performance of the requested act, as in the case of my request for you to read my manuscript.

My request implies consent when the requested act requires consent. Requesting is not consenting. They involve different normative powers. Consent releases someone from an obligation. Requesting creates a reason for action (or an obligation). The request serves as evidence that the requester has consented to the act in question. This principle applies to acts that require consent, not to those that do not.

Some requests create reasons, while others create obligation. It should be noted, however, that all requests create at least one specific obligation: the obligation to take the reasons they provide into account. The requestee is obliged to consider the reasons created by the requester, as disregarding them would be disrespectful to them. We owe it to others to consider the reasons they give us. We can treat these as request-dependent reasons and choose to honor the request. Alternatively, we can consider these reasons without honoring the request by explaining why we have declined the request and providing justification or context for our decision.

One last thing on the reason- and obligation-creating force of requests. We discussed Dan Khokhar's view that the reasons created by requests are grounded in special relationships. Let me clarify how such request-dependent reasons are rooted in the relationship between requester and requestee. Lewis refers to these as "relational reasons" (Lewis 2022, 239). For example, your request that your friend John talk with you about marital issues may create a reason for him only because you are friends; it would not create the same reason for a stranger. In other words, whether a request creates reasons depends on the normative structure of the relationship between the requester and the requestee, on what one owes to others as partners, friends, colleagues, neighbors, or fellow human beings.

Importantly, one does not need a special relationship with the requestee to create a reason through a request. We can create reasons for people we have never met, because we also owe certain forms of consideration to strangers. If a Japanese tourist, someone you have never met and will probably never see again, asks you for directions to the train station, you have a reason to help. This is something we owe each other as fellow human beings.

3.7 Enoch's account

Let me compare my account to the one put forward by David Enoch (Enoch 2011). Enoch thinks that requests are reason-giving in a, as already mentioned in Chapter 1, robust sense. They provide us with reasons in a robust sense by triggering already obtaining reasons of a particular kind (Enoch 2011, 9). Let me explain. The requester has the intention to give the requestee a reason to do as requested. By communicating her intention the requester gives the requestee a reason provided that there is a conditional reason which is triggered by the request. This is how this view is summarized by Enoch (Enoch 2011, 15):

(i) A intends to give B a reason to φ.
(ii) A intends B to recognize this intention;
(iii) A intends B's reason to φ to depend in an appropriate way on B's recognition of A's communicated intention to give B a reason to φ. (Enoch 2011, 15)

On this view the reason B has to φ depends on his recognition of the communicated intention.

Imagine that B recognizes A's intention to give him a reason to φ. B does so but she might have no reason to φ. The fact that B recognizes that A wants to give him a reason does not imply that B has a reason to φ. B might recognize A's intention to give her a reason to φ without taking A's request as a reason to act accordingly. Thus, it is not the intention that provides B with a reason to φ.

What then is it that provides B with a reason to φ on this account? What is it that fills the gap between intention to give a reason and actually giving him a reason? Enoch thinks that requests are triggering conditional reasons (Enoch 2011, 10). A asking B to do x, for instance, triggers the reason "if-A-asks-B-to do x-B has-a-reason-to-do x." A conditional reason of the form "if-A-asks-B to do x-B has-a-reason-to do x" already obtained before A asked B to do x. As the condition was satisfied, the reason was triggered and B had a reason to do x. The reason-giving force of requests depends on this view on a normative structure that is already in place. If there was no conditional reason the requests could have no reason-giving force.

Are requests triggering conditional reasons? I think that Enoch is right in thinking that a request gives us reasons against a background of a normative structure that is already in place. However, the normative structure is better captured in terms of request norms that already obtain. B has a reason to do x if and because the request norm applies when its conditions are met, namely, when A makes the request. The act of requesting activates the norm, thereby providing B with a reason for action. Before A asked, B had no such reason. After the request, B now has a reason to do x because the norm has come to apply.

This structure extends to other familiar norms. Consider, for example, "*You ought to help your partner if she needs help.*" This norm does not give you any reason to act unless your partner actually needs help. Once she does, the norm applies, and you thereby acquire a reason to help her, a reason you did not have before. The same is true of request norms: the request activates the norm and provides the requestee with a reason that was not previously in place.

This illustrates why requests are better understood as activating standing request norms rather than triggering conditional reasons. When A asks B to do x, B has a reason to comply because of a request norm: "If and because A asks B to do x, B has a reason to do x." This norm becomes applicable to B once A makes the request, and B should follow it because doing so is valuable or appropriate. This framework explains why A's request gives B a reason t act. By appealing to request norms, we can account for both the reason-giving force of requests and the conditions under which that force arises. Contrary to Enoch's view, requests do not trigger conditional reasons; rather, they create reasons insofar as they are grounded in the valuable features of what the requester is asking the requestee to do.

3.8 Requests for Future Favors

Requests can also create reasons for future actions. For example, Kate asks Jane to lend her bike in two weeks. Kate's request gives Jane a reason to do as requested at that future time.

However, if Kate no longer wants Jane's bike in two weeks, Jane would no longer be doing Kate a favor by lending her her bike. In this case, Jane would no longer have a reason to honor the request. Similarly, Kate could withdraw her request if she no longer needs the bike. By withdrawing a request, the request-dependent reason is removed. Her original request created a reason for Jane to lend her bike to Kate. Her withdrawal of the request eliminates the reason the original request has created.

Thus, Jane has a reason to comply with Kate's request at that future time if and only if:

a. the request is not withdrawn, and
b. the reasons to honor the request still apply to Jane (the requestee).

There may be situations in which the reasons for honoring a previous request no longer apply. Consider the following example. Paul has a drinking problem and asks Jed to ensure that he does not drink at a party on Saturday. Paul's request gives Jed a reason to act accordingly at that future time. However, at the party, Paul tells Jed that he has changed his mind, he no longer wants Jed to stop him from drinking. The reasons for honoring the original request no longer apply. They cease to apply once Paul no longer wants Jed to intervene and revokes his earlier request.

Does revoking an earlier request always eliminate the reasons for honoring the request? In the Paul/Jed case, once the request is revoked, Jed can no longer permissibly intervene on the basis of Paul's original request. Jed might still believe that sobriety is in Paul's best interest and treat that belief as an independent reason to stop him from drinking. However, the request-dependent reason appears to have been removed.

But is this always the case? This issue is also relevant in the context of revoking consent to "Ulysses contracts" (see Franklin-Hall 2023). Like Odysseus, one can consent to an act that will occur in the future, even if at that later time, one no longer wishes for it to happen. Consent to such contracts takes effect at a future point, anticipating that the consenter may not want to be treated in the way they currently prefer. As with consent to Ulysses contracts, a request may retain normative force even after the requester attempts to revoke it. This holds in cases where the requester is not competent to withdraw the earlier request.

But when does this lack of competence arise? I will draw on the standard view of competence, which holds that a person is competent to consent or make a request if they are capable of making an informed and reasoned decision (see Buchanan and Brock 1990, chapter 1). As Franklin-Hall puts it, competence requires "the ability, in a given situation, to make an informed and reasoned decision guided by their own values and commitments - whether they actually do so or not" (Franklin-Hall 2023, 66). Having this ability includes

a. knowing what one is doing, and
b. being able to respond to the reasons one has for making or withdrawing a request.

Criterion (a) is met if the agent understands that she is asking the requestee not to do something she previously wanted the requestee to do. Criterion (b) holds if the agent can recognize and respond to the reasons she has when revoking her request. An agent is incompetent to withdraw a request if the reasons for making the request still hold, yet she is unable to recognize or act upon them.

Let us further examine criterion (b). The reasons Paul had to ask Jed for interference stem from his values and desires. These provide the reasons for asking Jed to interfere. If Paul's values and desires have not substantially changed—if no genuine change of mind has occurred—these reasons still obtain. One can only conclude that Paul has genuinely changed his mind if he can articulate the reasons behind his new desire and explain why he no longer aims to avoid the consequences of heavy drinking. The question is not whether Paul now prefers to drink but whether the values underpinning his earlier request have changed. This is true only if Paul can provide a coherent explanation that makes his new stance intelligible.

Suppose the reasons Paul had to ask Jed for interference still apply at the party, but Paul does not act on them. One might argue that Paul could still act on these reasons, even though he chooses not to. However, if Paul, in the grip of his urge to drink, could not have been persuaded to maintain his prior request—even when reminded explicitly of those reasons—he lacks the ability to make a reasoned decision. In this case, Paul is incompetent to revoke his earlier request. His earlier request would still have normative force and justify Jed's intervention.

3.9 The Strength of Request-Dependent Reasons

Requests create request-dependent reasons. Does the strength of the reason created by the request differ in various cases? One could argue that the reasons requests create have always the same weight (see Schaber 2021, 438). However, some requests seem to be more important than others. Take the case of my partner asking me to look after the children tonight. Imagine that at the same time, my neighbor asks me to do the same for his children. Both requests provide me with reasons for action. However, it seems my partner's request carries more normative weight for me than the neighbor's request.

What explains the normative difference? It can be explained by reference to the normative weight the request-independent reasons have. The fact that my partner wants me to look after the children gives me a stronger reason than the fact that my neighbor wants me to do the same. My partner's request has more normative weight because her desires and interests count for more for me than the desires and interests of my neighbor. Thus, the difference in normative weight is due to the normative weight of the request-independent reasons.

Weltman thinks that we should reject this view. He writes:

> It is implausible to think that all reasons based on requests have *exactly* the same weight. Surely requests about life and death matters involve reasons of different weight than requests about trivialities. (Weltman 2023, 401)

Weltman's critique seems somewhat odd to me because, on his epistemic view of requests, requests do not create additional reasons. Instead, requests can track the reasons favoring the requested action that already exist, independent of whether a request has been made. The varying normative weight of requests can be grounded only in features of the requested act that give the addressee reasons for action independent of the request itself. Therefore, Weltman should agree that the normative weight of requests is determined by the normative weight of the desires they express. Requests track reasons with different normative weights, but these reasons are not created by the requests themselves.

The reasons to honor a request differ depending on the normative weight of the desires expressed in the requests. For instance, you have a reason to help your neighbor move house, but you have a stronger reason to do the same for your friend. Your friend's desire for your help carries more normative weight than your neighbor's. Consequently, the request-independent reasons to help your friend move house are weightier than those for your neighbor.

Similarly, the request-dependent reasons created by your friend's and your neighbor's requests do not carry the same normative weight.[4] The weight of request-dependent reasons is shaped by the normative structure of the relationship between the requester and the requestee. For example, a request from your partner carries greater normative importance for you than one from your neighbor. As a result, your partner's requests provide you with stronger reasons to honor the request and to act out of respect for the neighbor's reason-giving authority. In other words, you have stronger reasons to fulfill a request from your partner than from a neighbor or a stranger. The strength of request-dependent reasons is determined by the normative structure of the relationship between the requester and the requestee, that is, by what we owe partners, friends, colleagues, neighbors, and strangers.

3.10 Requesting What You Are Obliged to Do

A asks B to do x. Suppose B is already obliged to do x. Do requests create reasons when the requestee already has an existing obligation to do what the requester wants? Consider this case: Jeff says to John, "Please stop insulting me." John is already obliged not to insult Jeff; this obligation exists independently of Jeff's request. John should not insult Jeff.

Thus, the speech act can be understood as a demand that calls John's attention to an existing obligation while asserting his right not to be insulted. Yet, one might think that the request also adds a reason not to insult Jeff. John is already obliged not to insult him, but Jeff's request provides an additional reason to uphold that obligation.

However, I do not think we should accept this view. Jeff's speech act—"Please stop insulting me" —does not create a new reason. Why? John should follow the norm of not insulting others, but not because he was asked to do so. If he refrained from insulting Jeff because Jeff asked him not to, he would be doing the right thing for the wrong reason. It is John's obligation not to insult Jeff, and this obligation exists regardless of whether he was asked.

Thus, there is no request norm of the form: "If and because Jeff asks John not to insult him, John should refrain." Instead, the relevant norm is simply "John should not insult Jeff." The speech act does not create an additional reason for John. If you are already obliged to do x, and you do x merely because you were asked, you would be acting for the wrong reasons. Therefore, it is not good to take a request as a reason to honor the request if you have an already existing obligation to do what the requester wants you to do.

3.11 The Reasons to Honor Requests

One last thing: As we have seen above, you can honor requests for different reasons. You can honor a request by acting on a request-dependent and request-independent reason. You can conform to a request by acting only on a request-independent reason. You can comply with a request by acting on a request-dependent reason. Which reasons should we act on in cases where we are asked to do or omit something?

Following Scanlon, I think that you cannot choose the reasons you act on. You act for a reason x if you believe that you have reason x. You comply with a request for request-dependent reasons if you believe that the request is a reason for you to do as requested. By contrast, you act only for a request-independent reason if you believe that this is your only reason to do as requested. As Scanlon puts it,

> When one sees several considerations as counting in favor of the same action, one cannot choose to act on one of them rather than another unless one downgrades some of the reasons by changing one's mind about whether they really do count … in favor of the action in question. (Scanlon 2008, 61)

If you cannot choose to act for a reason, you cannot choose to comply with a request for a request-dependent reason (we will come back to this point in Chapter 7). It is good to honor a request because you were asked to do so. It is also good to honor a request for request-independent reasons, for instance, because it is good for the requester. For instance, it would be good for me if my colleague commented on my draft, even if she did so only for reasons unrelated to my request. However, it would be better if she commented on my draft because I asked her to, that is, if she did so out of respect for my reason-giving authority, rather than merely because doing so would be beneficial. Acting on request-dependent reasons is preferable, even if one cannot choose to do so freely. Fulfilling a request adds value precisely because it honors my reason-giving authority.

There are cases where failing to honor a request because it was made cannot be criticized. However, there are also cases where such a failure can be criticized. Consider this. You expect your colleague you met at a conference to read the paper. You do not expect her to read it because you have asked her to do so. You do not have the kind of relationship to justify your expectation that she will also do it for you. You expect a close friend who is also doing philosophy to read it for you. It would be worse if your friend did not do it for you than if your colleague did it. It would be good if your colleague read it also for you (because you asked her to do it). But it would be less bad if she did not read it for you. Our reasonable normative expectations vary according to our relationship with the other person. Of course, your friend cannot choose to act for request-dependent reasons. We would nevertheless expect her to do it for you. As a friend, she should see the request-dependent reasons she has to comply with the request. You can criticize her for failing to see these reasons. If she only honors your request for request-independent reasons, she will not be the kind of friend you might take her to be. Close friends do each other favors because they were asked to do so. Your friend might not live up to this ideal of friendship, at least not with you, which could understandably lead to disappointment. For instance, if a friend got lost in Paris and you helped him just to impress others, your friend would likely be bothered, and rightly so. That is not how friends should be treated. Your friend may expect you to tell her the way because she asked you. If you help merely to impress others, you are not acting as a friend.

3.12 Summary

Requests sometimes create reasons for actions and sometimes obligations. A creates a reason for B to do x by asking B if it is good or at least not sufficiently bad to do *x* and good to take the request as a reason for action. In such a case, a request norm exists, stating: "If and because A asks B to do x, B has a reason to do x." A's request might also create an obligation for B to do x. The request norm in this case would take the form: "If and because A asks B to do *x*, B is under an obligation to do x." Whether A's request creates a reason or an obligation depends on the normative structure of the relationship between requester and requestee. B has an obligation to do *x* when asked by A if B has a general obligation to take care of the relevant matters. In such cases, A's request creates an obligation by specifying the general obligation that B already holds.

Requests also create reasons for future favors. The requester can eliminate these reasons by revoking the request, as long as she is competent at the time of revocation. Requests do not create reasons if the requestee is already obliged to perform the requested act because it would not be good if the requester fulfilled the obligation because she was asked. The reasons requests create differ concerning their normative weight. Their strength is determined by what we owe each other as partners, friends, neighbors, and strangers. Finally, we cannot choose the reasons why we honor requests. However, it is good if we honor them for request-dependent reasons. You have a reasonable expectation that partners or friends comply with your requests for request-dependent reasons. You do not expect a stranger to act like that, even though it would be good if she did.

4

Requests and Orders

Raz argues that requests, unlike orders, do not create obligations. On his view, requests communicate the intention to create a reason for the addressee. By contrast, orders communicate an intention to impose an obligation on the addressee. Requests leave it up to the addressee to honor the request. Orders aim at taking the matter out of the addressee's hands. Conflicting reasons should no longer be considered by the addressee. Raz writes:

> In requesting and in commanding the speaker intends the addressee to recognize the utterance as a reason for action. The difference is that a valid command (i.e. one issued by a person in authority) is a peremptory reason. We express this thought by saying that valid commands or other valid authoritative requirements impose obligations. (Raz 1986, 37)

Owens rejects Raz's account of the difference between requests and orders. Owens thinks that requests can also create obligations, even though not in the same way as orders create obligations. Owens writes:

> A command imposes an obligation on me by communicating the intention of hereby imposing an obligation … In making his request, Tim may intend to impose an obligation but communicating this intention to me would be mere imprudence and would do nothing to bind me. It is the nature of our friendship that turns his request into a demand (which makes it the case that I would be wronging him if I declined). (Owens 2012, 100)

I think that Owens is right. As I have argued in the previous chapter, requests sometimes create obligations. They do so when they specify general obligations the requestee has toward the requester. The request norm that is satisfied by the request tells the requestee that she is obliged to do as requested. However, obligations are normally not imposed by requests, but rather by orders (or commands). A imposes an obligation on B to do x by issuing an order that B ought to do x. But how does the obligation-creating force of orders differ from the obligation-creating force of requests? You can commit a wrong as well as wrong someone by not honoring a request. However, requests are not orders and create obligations not in the same way as orders do. To see clearly how requests and orders differ in this respect, we need to know how orders create duties and then compare the two accounts of creating obligations.

4.1 Overview

In this chapter, I will argue that the imposition of obligations on others can be explained by reference to *order norms.*[1] Order norms can be expressed as follows: "If and because A tells B that B ought to do x, B ought to do x." There are specific reasons for the existence of such norms. An order norm of this type exists when two conditions are met:

1. The order specifies a general obligation B already has.
2. A fulfills one of her own obligations by issuing the order for B to do x.

Consider the following example. The dean orders me to chair a committee. I have a general obligation to serve on university committees, and the dean's order specifies that obligation by telling me that I ought to chair a particular committee. This order would not be binding on someone with no general obligation to serve on university committees. Additionally, by issuing her order to me, the dean discharges her own obligation to organize university committees. Conversely, if a colleague without such responsibilities issued the same order, it would not be binding.

Thus, orders impose obligations on others if and only if they (a) specify a general obligation of the addressee and (b) serve as a way for the prescriber to fulfill her own obligation. Importantly, binding orders do not draw the addressee's attention to an already existing obligation. For example, when someone says "Do not harm me," the obligation not to cause harm already exists and is not created by this speech-act. In contrast, my obligation to chair a particular committee has been created by the dean's order. It is the result of an exercise of *practical authority.*

I argue that practical authority is exercised when someone creates an obligation for another person by fulfilling the conditions described above. Exercises of *practical authority* have to be distinguished from exercises of *theoretical authority.* Exercises of theoretical authority draw someone's attention to an already existing obligation (or an already existing reason). A has theoretical authority over B if and only if A's statement, "You ought to do x," provides B with a reason to believe that she ought to do x (see also Raz 1986, 29).

Requests and orders create obligations by specifying general obligations. However, requests are not made to impose obligations on the requestee. They allow the requestee to deliberate and weigh the request against other considerations. Moreover, the requester need not fulfill an obligation by asking someone to do her a favor. Consider this example. My friend asks me to help him move house. It might be my obligation to help him because of what I owe him as a friend. However, I am free to weigh this obligation against other reasons I might have for not helping him move house. Requests leave it up to the requestee to consider all reasons that apply to the requestee in the given situation. By contrast, orders are meant to suspend the addressee's judgment on the matter.

Let us now explore these points in greater detail. The chapter has eight parts. The first part distinguishes between theoretical and practical authority. The second part presents Raz's service conception of authority and argues that it cannot explain the difference between theoretical and practical authority. The third part shows that practical authority to impose obligations can be accounted for by order norms. Order norms have the form "If and because A tells B that B ought to do x, B ought to do x." They obtain if and because (a) the order specifies a general obligation the addressee has to fulfill and (b) the prescriber discharges an obligation by ordering the addressee to act in a certain way. The fourth part discusses the proposal that orders are binding only if the addressees have agreed to follow them. I argue that my obligation to serve on university committees might result from my agreement to the university's rules. However, the dean's order is binding regardless of whether my general obligation to serve on university committees is grounded in my agreement. The fifth part argues that solving coordination issues is also an exercise of practical authority and rejects Tadros's critique. The sixth part discusses the epistemic duties of those who receive orders and compares them to those of requestees. The seventh part concludes by summing up the main differences between how orders and requests create obligations.

4.2 Practical and Theoretical Authority

The person issues an order if she communicates the intention to impose an obligation on the addressee.[2] The prescriber does not need to have the intention to impose an obligation on the addressee. She just has to *communicate* the intention to do so. If the addressee takes the speech-act to be an order, she believes that the prescriber has the intention to place her under an obligation. But the prescriber might just pretend to have this intention.

It holds for giving orders (O):

> (O) Person A issues an order to B to do x if and only if A communicates the intention to place B under an obligation by issuing the order.

You can order someone to do something without succeeding in bringing about the normative change. As Raz puts it,

> One can give an order even if one lacks the normative power to do so … If the person giving the order does not have the normative power to do so then the order is not binding. The gangster is as able as the parent to give an order but only the latter has the normative power to do so. (Raz 1975, 100)

Person A succeeds in imposing an obligation on B if and only if A has the normative power to impose a duty on B to do x. Issuing a binding order is the exercise of a normative power.

Before I discuss the issue of when we have the normative power to issue binding orders, I will address the question of what it means to have an obligation to do x.[3] I take it that if you have an obligation to do x you do not have a mere reason to do x. As Owens puts it,

> I may have a good reason to buy Tim a very nice birthday present ... But I'm unlikely to feel obliged to do this ... One difference here is that I won't be blamed for failing to buy him a nice present but .... (Owens 2012, 99)

If you have an obligation to do something, you commit a wrong if you flout that obligation, and blame is warranted. However, if you simply have a reason to do something (but no obligation), failing to do it does not constitute a wrong, and you are not appropriately subject to blame. An obligation created by an order can be overridden by weightier normative considerations. For example, suppose you have an obligation to organize a birthday party, and I am expected to assist you. You order me to buy flowers for the event, thereby placing me under an obligation to do so. However, it might turn out that the circumstances create a conflicting obligation for me—such as saving the life of a traffic accident victim. In such a case, the latter obligation outweighs the former. I should save the victim's life, and the obligation you imposed on me should not be fulfilled in this situation.

This leads us to the definition of *practical authority.* You have practical authority over another person if and only if you can change the reasons and obligations that apply to the addressee by exercising a normative power. You can change the reasons another person has either by making a request or by issuing an order. It thus holds for practical authority (PA):

> (PA) A has practical authority over B if and only if A can impose a duty on B by issuing an order or create reasons for action for B by making a request.[4]

Theoretical authority has to be distinguished from practical authority. Here is what I take theoretical authority to be (TA):

> (TA) A has theoretical authority over B if and only if A's ought statement "You ought to do x" is a reason for B to believe that she ought to do x (or has reasons to do x).

If the prescriber knows what the addressee ought to do, her orders are not reasons to act accordingly, but rather reasons to believe that she ought to do as told. As Heidi Hurd writes:

> The utterances of a theoretical authority provide reasons for belief, not reasons for action. They function, that is, evidentially. When a theoretical authority makes a claim concerning right action, its utterance provides a

> reason to think that there are other reasons (besides the sheer fact that the authority has spoken) to act as recommended. The prescriptions of such a theoretical authority are thus heuristic guides to detecting the existence and determining the probable truth of antecedently existing reasons for action. (Hurd 1991, 1615)

You can exercise theoretical authority either *by giving advice* or by *demanding something. Giving advice* aims at drawing attention to reasons the addressee has. When the doctor tells the patient that he should change his diet, she tries to draw his attention to reasons for action that apply to him. If the doctor is right about the reasons the patient has, his utterance is a reason for the patient to believe that he should change his diet. The doctor has theoretical authority over the patient if her advice is a reason for belief.

Thus it holds for advice (A):

> (A) A's communicative act "You ought to x" is advice if and only if the communicative act aims at drawing the addressee's attention to reasons for action that apply to her.

Giving advice is an exercise of theoretical authority if the communicative act "You ought to do x" is a reason for the addressee to believe that she has a reason to do x. Following the advice is not owed to the adviser. Following a demand is often owed to the one who makes the *demand*. It might also be owed to a third party.

Demands aim at drawing the attention of the addressee to some obligation of hers. Many speech-acts we take to be orders are in fact demands.[5] If Jill says to Kate "Don't hurt me" Jill draws Kate's attention to the fact that Kate is under an obligation not to hurt Jill. The obligation not to hurt others is not created by Jill's order. Her order makes the obligation explicit. Advice and demands both aim at tracking already existing obligations and reasons.

However, they are not the same, particularly in two respects: (a) how they relate to blame and (b) how they relate to the norms to which they draw the addressee's attention. Consider (a) first: when A advises B that she ought to do x, A either lacks the standing to blame B for not doing x or signals that she will not blame B if B fails to act accordingly. For example, a doctor advising you to quit smoking lacks the standing to blame you if you don't. Similarly, a friend who advises you not to cheat on your partner may have the standing to blame you, but makes it clear that he will not, even if you act wrongly. In contrast, A's statement that B ought to do x counts as a demand if A both has the standing to blame B for not doing x and communicates that she will blame B if B fails to comply.

As concerns b): When you demand that someone do x, you are not merely informing them about reasons or obligations that apply to them. Rather, you are taking a stand in support of a norm or a right. For example, if you demand that your colleague stop insulting you, you are asserting and standing up for your right not to be insulted. By contrast, if you say, "I think you should stop insulting my friend," and mean it as advice, you are not standing up for her rights, you are simply pointing out what he ought to do, perhaps for prudential reasons (e.g., "You should stop if you don't want to get into trouble").

It holds for demands (D):

> (D) A's communicative act "You ought to do x" is a demand if and only if it aims to draw the addressee's attention to an obligation she has and does so by asserting a norm or a right.

Demands are exercises of theoretical authority if and because they draw the addressee's attention to an existing obligation she has. A might falsely believe that B ought to do x. Her speech-act "You ought to do x" would then not be the exercise of theoretical authority but only an attempt to exercise it. Only legitimate demands are exercises of theoretical authority.

Some speech-acts may appear to be orders but turn out to be demands. Consider this case: John tells Paul, "Be quiet." This might initially be taken as an order—Paul should be quiet because John told him to. However, upon closer examination, John's speech-act is actually a demand. Suppose that, all things considered, Paul ought to be quiet. In that case, John's speech-act serves to draw Paul's attention to the fact that he should be quiet, rather than imposing an obligation. It is not John's command that makes it the case that Paul ought to be quiet; rather, certain features of the situation independently determine this obligation.

Thus, John's speech-act turns out to be a demand, highlighting an obligation that already exists rather than creating one. In this scenario, John possesses theoretical authority over Paul regarding the matter, provided that Paul indeed ought to be quiet based on the balance of reasons. This raises the question: What does it take to have practical authority over another person?

4.3 The Service Conception of Practical Authority

On Raz's service conception of practical authority, A has authority over B if A's orders or, as he puts it, "directives" make it more likely that B conforms to the reasons that apply to her. It is what Raz calls "the normal justification thesis":

> *It claims that the normal way to establish that a person has authority over another person involves showing that the alleged subject is likely better to comply with reasons which apply to him (other than the alleged authoritative directives) if he accepts the directives of the alleged authority as authoritatively binding and tries to follow them, rather than by trying to follow the reasons which apply to him directly.* (Raz 1986, 53)

That orders enable the addressee better to comply with reasons that apply to her could be true of exercises of practical as well as of exercises of theoretical authority. Exercises of theoretical authority create reasons for normative beliefs. Do exercises of practical authority create reasons to do as one has been told to do? Raz argues that orders do not add any additional first-order reasons. He writes:

> The fact that an authority requires performance of an action is a reason for its performance which is not to be added to all other relevant reasons when assessing what to do but should exclude and take the place of some of them. (Raz 1986, 13)

On Raz's view exercises of practical authority create second-order reasons. The second-order reasons are reasons to disregard the first-order reasons that speak against performing the act. The order should be taken "as an exclusionary reason to disregard some or all conflicting reasons for action" (Raz 1975, 83):

> Those subject to the authority are not allowed to second-guess the wisdom or advisability of the authority's directives. (Raz 2009, 140)

According to this view, it holds: If A has authority over B, A draws B's attention to the reasons and obligations B already has, thereby enabling B to better comply with them. Orders do not create first-order reasons but rather second-order reasons to disregard conflicting ones.

There are many issues to be discussed here. What are exclusionary reasons? How are they brought about by orders? However, I will not discuss these questions.[6] I would like to focus on the issue of whether Raz's claim that "the normal way to establish that a person has authority over another person involves showing that the alleged subject is likely better to comply with reasons which apply to him (other than the alleged authoritative directives) if he accepts the directives of the alleged authority as authoritatively binding" (Raz 1986, 53) provides us with an adequate picture of practical authority.

On Raz's view, A has practical authority over B if B likely better complies with the reasons that apply to him if she follows A's orders. The difficulty with this proposal is this: it cannot account for the difference between practical and theoretical authority. A has authority over B in cases where she draws B's attention to the reasons that apply to B as well as in cases where A creates reasons for B. Take an exercise of theoretical authority. Someone tells you that you should not hurt others. The prescriber helps you to conform with the reasons you already have not to hurt others. The same holds for someone who tells you that you ought to stop smoking. She draws your attention to reasons that already apply to you, and helps you to follow these reasons. The latter is an example of advice, and the former of a demand. Neither advice nor demands create duties or reasons.

Advice and demands both track reasons and obligations. By contrast, if someone imposes an obligation on you, you ought not to do something you already should have done before the order that imposed the obligation on you was issued. The service conception thus has difficulties in distinguishing theoretical and practical authority. The explanation of authority the service conception provides us with accounts for theoretical, not practical authority. Thus, another explanation of how obligations can be imposed on others, which is of practical authority, is needed.

4.4 Order Norms

The prescriber needs to have practical authority to issue orders to be able to impose obligations on the addressee. Here is a proposal for how someone might have the required authority. Consider the case of the dean telling me to chair a university committee, which I will take as a *paradigm case* of a binding order. I ought to chair the committee because the dean told me to do so. The dean is the person who has the authority to select the members and chairs of the university committees. Does the dean's order impose an obligation on me? If that was the case, I would have an obligation to chair the committee because she told me to do so. I argue that the following is happening here.

First, there might have been reasons for me to chair the committee before she ordered me to do so. However, the dean did not track an obligation that already existed before I was told by her to chair the committee. What happens in this case can be explained by order norms. Order norms are norms of the form "You ought to do x if and because A tells you to do x." The order norm in the dean's case tells us that "Members of staff ought to chair university committees if and because the dean tells them to do so."

Second, there are reasons for having such a norm. Consider the order norm "If and because the dean tells you that you ought to serve on a committee you ought to do it." As a member of staff, you have a general obligation to serve certain university interests, for instance, the interests that are served by you chairing a university committee. The dean's order specifies your general obligation. By specifying the general obligation she determines the content of the obligation. The specified—unlike the general—obligation is something you can follow. You ought to follow the specified obligation of chairing the committee in question. It is a binding order.

Why? The dean has the obligation to organize the university committees. Ordering you to chair the committee is a form of discharging her duty to organize the university committees. It is binding for you because you have a general obligation to serve the interests of the university that are served by your chairing the committee. The dean's order is only binding if it is a way of discharging some obligation of her own. If no obligation were discharged by the order, no obligation would have been imposed on you. For example, if your colleague ordered you to chair the committee, you would not be obliged to do so. The dean discharges her obligation to organize the university committees by ordering members of staff to serve on committees or to chair them. There is an order norm "If the dean tells you that you ought to chair the committee, you ought to chair the committee" if and only if the order is a way of discharging an obligation the dean has and a specification of a general obligation you have as a member of staff.

Order norms do not presuppose institutional settings. Consider the following case. You have an obligation to organize a birthday party for your partner. Friends and members of the family must do their share in making the birthday party possible. You order one of them to buy flowers for the party. Given that this is a way of discharging your obligation to organize the party and the addressee has to do her share, you issue a binding order that imposes an obligation on the addressee to do what you ordered to do, namely, to buy flowers for the party.

Thus, there is an order norm of the form "B ought to do x if and because A tells B that B ought to do x" if two conditions are met. (a) A's order specifies a general obligation B has and b) issuing the order to do x is a way of discharging an obligation A has. The content of the obligation to be fulfilled is determined by the specification.

Thus, the following applies to order norms (ON):

> (ON) If A tells B that B ought to do x, B ought to do x if and only if a) A's speech-act specifies a general obligation B has and b) discharges an obligation A has.

Orders serve as a means of discharging the obligations of those who issue them, provided they help bring about the outcome the prescriber is obliged to achieve—in this case, the organization of the university committees. An order is only binding if both conditions are met. Imagine that condition (a) was not met. Consider the following example. My colleague, who is also a member of staff, orders me to chair the university committee in question. This would not constitute a binding order. Why? While I do have a general obligation to serve on committees, my colleague has no obligation to organize university committees and, therefore, lacks the authority to impose such an obligation on me. By contrast, the dean has the obligation to organize the university's committees, which gives her the authority to issue binding orders requiring staff members to serve on them. As concerns condition (b), imagine the dean ordered you to clean up her office. By issuing her order, she would neither specify an obligation you have nor discharge an obligation of hers, and thus she would not impose an obligation on you.

You ought to chair the committee because the dean told you to do so. The ought is created by the dean's order. Her order satisfies the conditions of the order norm. The order norm "You ought to chair a committee if the dean tells you to do so" already exists. However, it does not give me any reasons if the dean has not yet satisfied the conditions of the norm by telling me to chair the committee. The dean's order does not track an already existing obligation because there is no such obligation ("You ought to chair this committee") to be tracked by the order. Moreover, the order would not impose an obligation on someone if no order norm was already in place. The order norm enables the dean to impose an obligation on particular persons.

Compare this to an exercise of theoretical authority. Jill tells Kate not to hurt her. Kate ought not to hurt Jill, regardless of Jill's speech-act. Kate should refrain from hurting Jill, not because Jill told her, but because it is the right thing to do. Similarly, you ought to chair the university committee because the dean ordered you to do so. However, you would not be obliged to chair it if the dean had not given the order.

The proposed account of practical authority can explain how the dean is able to impose an obligation on me and also why the dean has the authority to impose obligations on the members of staff. The authority of the dean is part of the order norm. "As a member of staff of your university, you ought to chair a committee if and because the dean tells you to do so." The order norm determines who has the authority to satisfy the condition of the norm and also which acts the authority applies to. "You ought to satisfy a specified obligation if it is issued by the person who discharges one of her obligations by issuing orders of this kind."

The proposed account of practical authority also explains why certain order norms need an institutional setting. The order norm ("You ought to do what the dean tells you to do if and because the dean tells you to do x") can only be followed if there is a dean. Other order norms, however, might not need such an institutional setting.

Consider a slightly modified birthday example. John tells his brother to buy flowers for the upcoming birthday party of their mother John is supposed to organize. John's order imposes an obligation on his brother to buy flowers, given that his brother has a general obligation to do his share in organizing the party and John has the obligation to organize the whole event. No institutional setting is required here. What is required is that John has an obligation to organize the event, and that an order norm exists, stating "John's brother ought to buy flowers if John tells him to do so for the birthday party he is about to organize."

The proposed account can also explain how an order can fail to impose an obligation even though the prescriber performs a communicative act intending to impose an obligation on the addressee of the order. The order fails to impose an obligation if it does not discharge an obligation the prescriber has or if it does not specify an obligation the addressee has. For instance, John's order fails to impose an obligation if he has no obligation to organize the party or if his brother is not obliged to do his share.

One might wonder how the proposed account can deal with orders that tell me to do something I should not do. Do I have to follow the dean's order even if I should not do what she orders me to do? Say, I do not have the required competence to chair the committee in question. She should have chosen a colleague who has the required competence. Does it still hold that I ought to chair the committee? It seems that this is what the idea of having practical authority over others implies. Scott Shapiro argues that "practical authorities claim the right to obligate even when they are wrong" (Shapiro 2000, 27). And he thinks that a theory of practical authority has to account for this fact. Is the given account of practical authority able to do so?

Is the order norm satisfied if the dean makes a mistake? Take the case just mentioned. Would the dean's order still impose an obligation on me? I think it would still place me under an obligation to chair the committee. Her order specifies a general obligation I have. She discharges her obligation to organize the university committees by ordering me to chair a particular committee. Whether the dean issues a binding order depends on whether the order is a way the dean discharges her obligation to organize the university committees. I ought to chair the committee, provided the ought created by the dean is not defeated by conflicting obligations I have to fulfill toward the university or other persons. If I have an obligation toward the university in this case that defeats my obligation to chair the committee, I would be justified in refusing to chair the committee. Still, I would have a *pro tanto obligation* to chair the committee, a defeated obligation to chair the committee. An obligation has been created if the two conditions mentioned above are met. Another obligation might turn out to be more important. However, refusing to chair the committee needed to be explained; I might even have reasons to apologize for not doing it. The point is that the dean's order imposes an obligation on me, even if she should have imposed this obligation on someone else, and even if I'm under a conflicting weightier obligation. If I have a conflicting weightier obligation, due to competence-related reasons, not to chair the committee, then I should not do it. However, I would still have a pro tanto obligation to chair the committee—an obligation that would be defeated by the weightier one. I may owe the dean an explanation for flouting the obligation to chair the committee. In other words, the dean imposes an obligation on me as long as she satisfies the relevant order norm. The obligations she thereby creates need, however, not be indefeasible.

4.5 Agreements

Alternatively, one could think that the obligation to chair the committee has not been created by the dean satisfying an order norm, but rather by the fact that I have agreed to follow her orders when I joined the university. Andrei Marmor advocates this view. He writes:

> I am bound to comply with the dean's instructions because I have agreed to do so; subjection to the authority of the dean is just part of the deal I made when I joined the institution. To be sure, I am not assuming here that the consent or agreement that binds me is one I have made with the dean or with any other particular official in the university. (Marmor 2011, 354)

The thought is this: When I joined the university I agreed to follow the orders of whoever the dean will be. My agreement put me under an obligation to do what the dean tells me to do, provided that university matters are concerned. To take our example again: because I agreed to do so when joining the university, I ought to chair the committee when told by the dean. Her order triggers an obligation of mine. I'm under an obligation to follow her orders. She orders me to chair a particular committee. I thus should chair this committee. The obligation she triggers by her order is not created by her, but rather by me. I created the obligation to follow her orders by agreeing to do so when I joined the university.

There are two reasons, however, to prefer the view that my obligation to chair the committee is not based on a prior agreement but rather on the fact that I'm a member of staff. (a) First, it is not clear whether I agreed to follow the dean's orders. That is to say, it is not clear whether I did anything while I joined the university that put me under a duty to follow the dean's orders. It seems more plausible to say that I knew that this would be one of the obligations I would have as a member of staff. I will be under these obligations because I am a member of staff and not because I agreed to be obliged to comply with the dean's orders.

(b) Second and more importantly, it is not clear whether this view of practical authority can account for various forms of people having practical authority. Take the birthday case I have mentioned. John does not need his brother's agreement to impose an obligation on him to buy flowers. As a member of the family, his brother has a general obligation to do his share in organizing the birthday party of their mother. Or take the case of a parent who tells her adolescent son to stay at home tonight. If these are binding orders they are unlikely to be created by any agreement given by the addressees of the orders.

However, even if my obligation to chair the committee was grounded in my agreement to follow the dean's orders, the binding nature of her orders stems from her obligation to organize university committees and my obligation to serve the university's interests through committee work. The dean's order for me to chair the committee in question is binding because it fulfills her obligation to organize committees while specifying my general obligation to support the university's objectives in a specific manner. The relevant order norm might be grounded in an agreement. However, the order norm explains how an obligation is imposed on me.

4.6 Coordination Norms

One may also impose duties on others by resolving coordination problems. Consider the classic example. People have to drive either on the right or the left. All drivers ought to drive on the same side of the road. Their driving behavior needs to be coordinated to avoid harm and death. The government is obligated to solve the coordination problem and decides that the drivers ought to drive on the right. Thus, they ought to drive on the right because they have been told by the government to do so. They were not under an obligation to drive on the right before the government told them to drive on the right. The government could have told them to drive on the left. They then would have had the obligation to drive on the left. It thus seems that the order of the government imposes the obligation on them to drive either on the right or on the left. They ought to do what they have been told to do by the government.

Tadros argues that we do not impose any obligations on people by solving coordination problems (Tadros 2020). Here is the main reason why he thinks that this is not the case. I ought to drive on the right or the left. I ought to do the same as others do. If they drive on the right I should also drive on the right. The order the government issues that people should drive on the right is a reason for me to believe that others will drive on the right. They will think that this is the way to prevent them from harming others and being harmed by others. Thus, they will drive on the right. The fact that they will drive on the right places me under an obligation to drive on the right too. Tadros writes:

> As they are well motivated, each will do this, simply because that will save the lives of more (people), and that is what they are required to do. (Tadros 2020, 83)

Tadros is right, I ought to drive on the right if this is what all others do because that will protect people from being harmed and killed. But the order is still imposing an obligation on citizens to drive on the right. Consider the following example. Say the government tells people to drive on the right. The government is extremely unpopular, and people tend to ignore its orders. Sometimes they do the opposite of what they have been told by the government. Imagine that in the traffic case you have good evidence that the others will drive on the left. They want to do the same as the others do, but they want to defy the government's order. You have good reason to believe that they will drive on the left. Then, of course, you ought to drive on the left too. You should do what others will do if doing so avoids causing considerable harm to others. The order of the government gives you evidence of what others will do. In the defiance case, it provides you with evidence that others will do the opposite of what the government tells them to do, which then imposes an obligation on you to do the opposite as well.

However, by solving a coordination problem, the government imposes an obligation on you. It is the government's responsibility to address coordination problems. Citizens have a general obligation to coordinate their actions, and the government is tasked with specifying how this obligation should be fulfilled. In the case at hand, a conflict arises: the obligation created by the government clashes with the obligation not to harm others. In such cases, the obligation not to harm others may override the obligation imposed by the government. Nonetheless, the government's directive—such as the order to drive on the right—would remain binding, a pro tanto obligation.

To sum up, it is important to distinguish between exercises of theoretical authority and practical authority. Exercises of theoretical authority do not impose duties on those addressed, whereas exercises of practical authority do. Unlike theoretical authority, practical authority operates under norms such as "If and because person A tells you that you ought to do x, you ought to do x." For example, if the dean orders me to chair a committee, I am obliged to do so. Her order places me under an obligation if it aligns with the relevant order norm—which it does, provided that I have a general obligation to serve on university committees and the dean has an obligation to organize them.

4.7 Blameworthiness

You should not comply with orders that are not binding, nor should you honor requests that are defeated by request-independent reasons. You would be blameworthy if you followed orders you should not follow, or requests where compliance would be wrong. For example, if an officer orders a soldier to mistreat a prisoner of war, the soldier should refuse to comply. He might be forced to follow the order, but he should not if he has a choice. Similarly, when John asks Fred to help spread lies about a colleague, Fred should refuse the request and would be culpable if he honored the request. You are blameworthy for honoring a request you ought not to. But does the same apply to orders? Are you blameworthy for following an order you should not follow, provided that you have a choice? I believe that requests and orders differ in this regard. I believe that we are always blameworthy for honoring inappropriate requests, but not for following inappropriate orders.

Consider an employer who orders an employee to fix his car. The employer is not discharging any obligation by giving this order, as this is not part of the employee's responsibilities. The employee should not comply, but would he be blameworthy if he did (assuming that he had a choice)?

It may be obvious to the addressee of an order that the order does not entail an obligation. In such a case, the addressee should refuse to follow it. However, if the addressee is uncertain about whether the order is binding, must she investigate further? Orders are typically intended to be followed without additional consideration. As Raz argues, the addressee of an order should not evaluate the situation on its merits but should proceed directly to act (Raz 1975, 193). If it is clear that the order is not binding, the addressee should refuse to comply. However, if this is not obvious, she may follow the order without further deliberation.

The point is that the epistemic duties of receivers of orders differ from those of requestees. Requestees may consider all reasons for and against honoring the request. They are not expected to follow the request without weighing pros and cons. In contrast, the recipient of an order does not have to weigh all the reasons for and against compliance. In certain pressing cases, doing so could even be wrong. The addressee of an order simply needs to ensure she does not act against obvious reasons that would advise against following the order. She does not need to assess every reason, because, as Owens suggests, "the order is there to pre-empt deliberation … the order should exclude at least some of the considerations that recommend disobedience from your practical deliberation" (Owens 2012, 86). The addressee of the order may proceed to comply and might even be required to do so. In contrast, a requestee who fails to consider whether there are good reasons not to honor a request risks committing a wrong for which she could be blamed. Requests are not meant to exclude considerations of noncompliance from deliberation. The requester leaves it up to the requestee to weigh all reasons for and against honoring the request and to make up her own mind.

Owens does not share this view. He believes that requests and orders are similar in their role in shaping practical deliberation. He writes:

> If I am requested to do something, then it makes sense for me to do it without my deliberating about whether to do it, without my weighing pros and cons. (Owens 2012, 86)

It may not make sense to weigh the pros and cons if it is obvious that the request is backed by reasons, but if it is not clear whether you should honor the request, it makes sense to deliberate. However, the requester does not want you to suspend judgment. Unlike orders, requests do not exclude considerations that recommend noncompliance from your deliberation. The requester leaves it up to the requestee to decide whether to honor the request and does not intend to take that decision out of the requestee's hands. You are, therefore, blameworthy if you honor a request you should not have honored. It only makes sense to honor a request without my weighing pros and cons if it is obvious that you should honor the request. You remain blameworthy for honoring an improper request, even if it was not immediately clear that the request should have been refused. Your obligation to ensure that a request is legitimate is more demanding than your obligation to resist following an order that is wrong. Compliance with a request is your responsibility. However, following an order you should not follow is only blameworthy if it was obvious that you should have refused it.

4.8 Summary

To sum up: Orders impose obligations on others if and only if they specify a general obligation that the addressee is required to fulfill and serve as a means for the prescriber to discharge her own obligation. Requests sometimes also create obligations. But they do not impose obligations the way orders do. Requests that create obligations also specify general obligations. However, the requester unlike the prescriber of an order does not need to discharge an obligation by requesting someone to do something. My partner is not obliged to decide who should care for the children, but her request for me to take on that responsibility creates an obligation for me. Requests create obligations by specifying a general obligation without thereby discharging an obligation of the requester.

The prescriber of an order intends to impose an obligation. This is not the intention of the requester. The requester might know that the requestee will be under an obligation to comply with the request, but she does not want to impose an obligation. This is why she believes that the requestee is allowed to consider the request in light of all reasons that apply to her. The requester does not want the requestee to move directly to honor the request. There is, from the requester's perspective, nothing wrong with taking your time to consider the request. By contrast, the prescriber of an order wants the addressee to execute the order, and the addressee would miss the point of the order if she started pondering the case in light of all the reasons that apply to her.

5

Requesting and Begging

In the preceding chapter, I have compared requests and orders. In this chapter, I will compare requesting with begging. By asking your colleague "Could you please read my draft!" you might not make a request but beg her to do something for you. We can ask others to do us a favor, we can also beg them to do so. Begging and requesting are not the same. But they are both addressing others to get them to do what we want them to do. I beg my colleague to read my draft because I want her to do so. However, by begging others to do something we address others differently. How do requesting and begging differ? And do they have a different normative force? Does my begging unlike my requests not create reasons for action? How begging differs from making requests is the topic of this chapter.

Begging did not get much attention in the philosophical literature. Requesting is usually compared to commands but not to begging others. A reason for this might be that begging has a bad reputation. Khokhar who is one of the few who deals with begging gives a reason why it might have a bad reputation by arguing that begging is inherently demeaning (Khokhar 2022). If this was the case, it would be quite natural to think that it has no normative force.

5.1 Overview

Does begging have no normative force? In this chapter, I argue that begging can have normative force. Like requests, begging can sometimes create reasons for action. However, it differs from requesting in two significant respects: (a) begging typically, though not always, expresses more intense desires, and more importantly, (b) when one begs, one does not wish to leave the decision entirely up to the other person. Begging creates a reason for action when acting accordingly would be good or at least not sufficiently bad, and when it is good to treat the act of begging itself as a reason. In such cases, it is good to do what someone wants you to do specifically because they have begged for it.

One might argue that begging has no normative force because it is *inherently demeaning* and, for that reason, should never be taken as a reason for action. This perspective might regard begging as inherently demeaning because it takes the beggar to relate to others as inferior. However, I contend that begging is not always demeaning. There are situations in which begging expresses an intense desire without positioning the beggar as inferior to others.

Let us explore these points in greater detail. The chapter has four parts. The first part shows how requesting and begging differ. The second part criticizes Khokhar's idea that begging is inherently demeaning. The third part deals with the normative force of begging. I argue that begging creates reasons for action if it is good or at least not sufficiently bad to do the desired act and if it is good to perform the act because one was begged to do so. The fourth part concludes.

5.2 How Requesting and Begging Differ

We beg others to do something in order to persuade them to act. If you beg your colleague to do you a favor, it is because you really want or need her to do it. This is what begging and requesting have in common. But how should begging be understood? The *Oxford Dictionary* defines begging as asking "somebody for something … in an anxious way because you want or need it very much," The term "begging" is used in various contexts, and no single definition captures the full nature of the act. However, a second personal address would not be considered begging unless what you are asking for is portrayed as highly necessary or as something that should be carried out without further deliberation. So, how does begging differ from making a request?

Begging is a form of requesting. When A begs B to do x, A communicates an intention to give B a reason to do x. However, begging differs from standard requesting in two ways. (a) Begging typically, though not always, conveys a more intense desire than a simple request. Consider the following example. You have written a paper and urgently need expert feedback. You say to your colleague John, "Please, John, could you read my paper today? It's really urgent and important to me." In this case, you are begging John to read your paper. This is not a standard request; it conveys an intense desire and emphasizes urgency and importance. By contrast, a standard request such as "I'd be happy if you have time to read my paper" lacks this intensity and sense of urgency.

Begging typically expresses intense desires, though not in all cases. The main difference between requesting and begging is this: (b) When you beg someone to do something, you do not want to leave it as open to the addressee to decide whether to comply, as you would with a request. Consider Khokhar's "Car Ride" case:

> *Car Ride*: Reckless and Passenger are driving together on an icy winter night. Reckless is joyfully speeding and swerving, nearly causing the car to slide off the road. Passenger says Reckless should really slow down. Reckless ignores this advice, prompting Passenger to continue, "I'm begging you, please slow down or you'll get us killed!"

In this case, the driver should immediately slow down, without weighing any other reasons to act differently. From the beggar's perspective, no other reasons justify considering an alternative course of action. The reasons for the driver to slow down clearly take precedence. The person begging may be mistaken about the reasons that apply to the addressee, but they view the reasons for the addressee to act accordingly as overriding any conflicting reasons. The beggar wants the addressee to treat the begging as if it were an order, in the sense that conflicting reasons should be disregarded. However, the beggar does not have the intention to impose an obligation on the addressee. This may be because doing so could be counterproductive, as the addressee might not respond well to an order. The message conveyed through begging is still "It's up to you to do what I want," rather than "I am imposing a duty on you to act as I want." The addressee is told that it is ultimately her choice, but that she should not consider conflicting reasons. Begging is not intended to function like an order.

The question remains: Does begging nevertheless create an obligation? Isn't the driver obliged to slow down after being begged by the passenger?

5.3 Inherently Demeaning?

Before we deal with the normative force of begging, we have to address another issue that has been raised by Khokhar. Khokhar argues that begging is—unlike requesting—a form of relating to others as an inferior. He argues "that begging is both a unified and protean phenomenon. It's unified in that the activity is inherently demeaning because it constitutively involves relating to another as an inferior, rather than equal, as a means of motivation" (Khokhar 2022, 28). Begging is taken by Khokhar as an attempt to motivate someone to do something by addressing her not as an equal but rather as subject to the others' mercy. Khokhar illustrates the demeaning character of begging with the "Car ride" (where Passenger begs Driver to slow down, see above) and the "Breakup" example:

> *Breakup*: Husband and Wife have had significant problems in their marriage for some time. They've tried addressing their issues in multiple ways including a great deal of marriage counseling. The problems persist and Wife eventually says to Husband, *"I tried so hard but I can't do it anymore. I'm leaving you."* Husband kneels in response and says *"Please don't leave, I'm begging you"* (Khokhar 2022, 29)

How are these two forms of begging supposed to be demeaning? Let us consider first the Car ride case. Khokhar argues that the demeaning character of this case is best explained "by the way the beggar refrains from claiming what they have a right to, in a way that expresses that they don't have a right to it" (Khokhar 2022, 31). The demeaning character of the begging in the Breakup example needs a different explanation because Husband does not have the right to make his Wife stay with him. Khokhar holds that the demeaning character of the begging can be seen by reference to "what Husband forgoes in opting for it" (Khokhar 2022, 32). He did not try to convince her to stay and he did not accept her decision and said "I want to stay together but I understand that won't work for you" (Khokhar 2022, 32). Both acts of begging are demeaning, but they are demeaning for different reasons. Other acts of begging might be demeaning again for other reasons. However, they are all—on Khokhar's view—inherently demeaning.

Is this true? One could say that begging is demeaning if the one who is begging acts as if her desires and interests were less important than those of the addressees or as if she would not have the same rights. Khokhar suggests that this is what you do when you beg others to do something for you. However, I believe that begging does not have to be demeaning, and the person begging need not see her desires and interests as less important, nor herself as someone with fewer rights than others. Consider the car ride case again. Say, Passenger first asks Driver to slow down. Driver ignores her request. Driver wrongs her by doing so. Passenger still feels uncomfortable and wants Driver to slow down. The only way for Passenger to stop his reckless speeding is - it seems - to communicate her fear and her intense desire that Driver slows down. This form of begging would not have a demeaning character. Of course, Passenger should not be forced to beg Driver to slow down, and Driver is to be blamed for ignoring Passenger's request. However, Passenger does not relate as an inferior to Driver if she communicates how she feels and that she really wants Driver to slow down. This form of begging would not be demeaning.

The same holds for the Breakup example: Instead of begging her to stay Husband should have tried to convince her to do so. Or he should have said, "I understand your decision; nevertheless, I would be happy if you stayed." But he begged her to stay. Again, he does not relate to her as an inferior if his begging is just about expressing his anxiety that she will leave and his intense desire that she will stay. He does not take himself as not having the same rights nor as someone whose desires and interests count for less than those of others. He just expresses his authentic anxiety that she will leave him. Even if it was wrong to beg her, it was not demeaning. Thus, not all acts of begging are inherently demeaning. Begging is demeaning if it is an expression of not considering yourself as having the same rights. If Passenger said to Driver, "I know that my voice does not count, but I beg you slow down," Passenger would indeed relate to Driver as an inferior. However, not all forms of begging are like that. Begging is not "a request made against the backdrop of a normatively concerning power asymmetry."[1] You beg John to read your paper, but there is no power asymmetry between you and John. You simply express how urgently you need his feedback.

5.4 The Normative Force of Begging

Does begging, like requesting, sometimes create reasons for action and sometimes obligations? The answer to this question is similar to the one given above regarding the reason- and obligation-creating force of requests. Begging creates reasons and possibly also obligations if there are begging norms. They have the form "If and because A begs B to do x, B ought to do x." The ought can be understood in terms of reasons or obligations. The begging norm "If and because A begs B to do x, B ought to do x" exists if the following two conditions are met: (a) It is good or at least not sufficiently bad that B does x, and (b) it is good that B does x because B has been begged by A to do so. The first condition (a) is met if it is true that doing x is good or not sufficiently bad. The second condition (b) is satisfied if taking A's begging as a reason to do x would be good.

If the begging falls under a begging norm, it creates a reason in the same way that requests do, and can therefore justifiably be taken as a reason to do what the person begging is asking. However, we would likely avoid saying, "I did it because she begged me," as this can carry a connotation of superiority. Instead, we might say, "She insisted," or "She implored me," since these expressions convey the same idea without suggesting a power imbalance.

Take this example. John begs Jill to lend him her bike as he otherwise will not make it for an important job interview ("Please can I take your bike, I really need it"). It is good to lend him her bike, he would otherwise miss a great job opportunity. And it would also be good if she did it because he begged her to do it. The corresponding begging norm would hold: "If and because John begs Jill to do something important to him, Jill ought to act accordingly."

A begs B to do x. It might (a) not be good to do x and it might (b) not be good to do x because A begged B to do so. A's begging creates a reason for B only if both conditions are met. It might be good to do x but not good to do x because B was asked to. Consider this. Paul begs Kate to read his draft. He implores her to read it: "Please read it, I will do anything you want me to do if you read it." It would be good if she read it but not because Paul begged her to do so. It might be inappropriate to beg her to read his draft.

Paul's begging might be inappropriate for various reasons. (a) It is not appropriate for Paul to beg Kate as her colleague. Instead, as a colleague, he may ask her to read his draft. That is, begging is not appropriate if the same aims can be achieved by simply asking someone to do what one wants them to do. Begging is, as Khokhar puts it, "bad … if the act of begging precludes or replaces valuable ways of interacting that the parties have reasons to care about in the context" (Khokhar 2024, 1434), and if those ways, I would add, also allow one to achieve the same aims. (b) Paul's begging might be inappropriate because reading the draft may not be as important or urgent as he portrays it. (c) It might also be inappropriate because Paul should leave it up to Kate to decide whether to read the draft. (d) Alternatively, it could be inappropriate if Paul has a right against Kate to read his drafts due to their mutual promise to do so. If one of these conditions is met, Paul's begging does not create a reason for Kate to do what he wants her to do.

If, however, the two conditions are met, Paul's begging creates a reason for Kate to read his draft. It might create a reason, it might also create an obligation. If it is very important to Paul that she reads it, and given that they often work together, Kate has not a reason but an obligation to read Paul's draft.

These conditions might rarely be met in cases of begging. This rarity may be grounded in the fact that the person begging should not have to beg for what she wants; she may have a right to it or should be able to ask for it. However, this does not mean that the two conditions are never fulfilled, only that they are likely to be met rarely (as, for instance, when I urgently need your feedback on my paper).

What is the normative force begging has in the two Khokhar cases? Passenger begs reckless Driver to slow down. Driver should not drive that fast in the first place. Does Passenger's begging add a reason for Driver to slow down? His begging expresses an intense desire, but it would not motivate Driver to slow down. The responsibility lies with Driver for driving too fast and disregarding Passenger's anxiety. Passenger should not have to beg for

Driver to reduce speed. The fact that Passenger is begging does therefore not create an additional reason for Driver to slow down, as it would not be good to treat it as such.

Consider again the Husband/Wife case. He begs her not to break up the marriage and to stay with him. Does his begging create a reason for her to stay? It seems obvious that she should not stay because he has begged to do so. Even if she has reasons not to break their marriage, it would be the wrong reason to stay. This is also what makes his begging inappropriate. Begging, like requesting, aims at providing the addressee with a reason to act in a certain way. But because Husband's begging cannot be the reason to do what Husband wants Wife to do, his begging is inappropriate. It cannot be successful right from the start.

5.5 Summary

Begging someone to do something is not the same as requesting someone to do something. Begging differs from requesting in two respects: (a) the desire the act of begging expresses is typically more intense than the desire request is bringing to the addressee's attention; (b) the act of begging aims at getting the addressee to move directly to perform the desired act. Acts of begging also create reasons for action. They do so if and only if it would be good or not sufficiently bad to perform the act and good to do it because the agent was begged to act accordingly.

6

When Requests Fail to Make a Normative Difference

Chapter 2 and Chapter 3 dealt with the issue of how requests create reasons and obligations. Not all requests, however, create reasons or obligations. Some fail to make a normative difference. They fail to make a normative difference when we do not have the practical authority to make a request. As I have argued in Chapter 4, you have practical authority over another person if and only if you are able to create reasons for her or impose obligations on her. When do we have the practical authority to create reasons by making requests? We are often not sure whether we have this authority. May I ask a colleague I never met to read my 300-page draft? May I ask my neighbor to help me to move house? Would it be okay to ask a colleague to talk to my partner about a marriage issue? When do we have the practical authority to make a request?

6.1 Overview

In this chapter, I will show when we lack the practical authority to create reasons for others by making requests. As I have argued in Chapter 3, requests create reasons if it is good or at least not sufficiently bad to do as requested and good to take the request as a reason. Honoring the request might not be good all things considered. The reasons to honor it might be defeated by conflicting reasons. Honoring the request might be too demanding for the requestee and therefore defeated by reasons of well-being. The requestee would then not be permitted, rationally or morally, to honor the request. She has a pro tanto reason to honor it but would not be permitted to do as requested, all things considered. In some instances, the requester might lack the authority to provide even pro tanto reasons for action by making a request. There are several reasons why we lack the authority to create reasons by making requests. Let us consider them one by one: (a) Your request fails to create a reason for someone to honor the request because you lack the necessary relationship with the person you are asking. For example, imagine you ask your neighbor to discuss a marital issue with your wife. Your request does not create a reason to act for your neighbor if he does not want to have the kind of relationship with you that would give such a request normative force. (b) A request may also fail to create a reason if and because it disrespects the requestee's social standing. For instance, asking the dean to clean your apartment does not give her a reason to do so; such a request would be disrespectful to her social standing as a dean. (c) We also lack the authority to create reasons for others if our request disrespects them as moral persons. This applies to requests that are humiliating or embarrassing for the requestee. (d) Finally, a request fails to make a normative difference if the requested action should not be performed simply because it was asked for, even if acting would benefit the requester. In such cases, the act might still be inappropriate when framed as a response to the request itself.

I will then turn to cases in which requests wrong the requestee. Laskowski and Silver argue that requests wrong requestees when they are disrespectful. I build on their view by arguing that requests wrong requestees when they violate rights that the requestee holds against the requester. While some requests are merely misplaced, others constitute genuine wrongs. Requests also fail to create reasons when they are accompanied by threats. In such cases, they can no longer be considered genuine requests. Additionally, deception causes requesters to falsely believe they have reasons to make requests when they do not. It also prevents people from making requests they have reasons to make.

Let us explore these issues in further detail. The chapter has six parts. The first part explains why we should sometimes refrain from exercising our normative power to create reasons by making requests, even when we possess that power. The second part addresses the authority to make requests, arguing that this authority depends both on the kind of relationship we seek with the requester and on the social and moral standing of the requestee.

The third part addresses the issue of whether requests can wrong requestees. I agree with Laskowski and Silver that this can be the case and argue that they do so by violating requestees' rights. The fourth part argues that requests accompanied by threats cannot be considered requests. The fifth part shows how deception can lead people to make requests they should not make. The sixth part concludes.

6.2 Reasons Not to Exercise Your Normative Power

What does it mean to have the authority to make a request? To have the authority to make a request is to have practical authority over another person, to be able to give her reasons for action or to impose duties on her. That is, A has practical authority over B if A is able to create reasons by making requests or to impose obligations by issuing binding orders. Let us focus on reason-creating requests. You may have the practical authority to create pro tanto reasons or all-things-considered reasons for complying with your request.

Let me begin with requests that, while capable of creating normative reasons, nevertheless *should not* be made. That is, you might have the normative power to create reasons by making a request, but you should refrain from exercising it. I have argued that in cases where a request creates reasons, the person receiving the request is obligated to weigh the reasons for and against honoring the request. However, you should not create such a reason by making a request when the burden of this obligation would be too great for the requestee. Consider the following case: Dan needs a kidney transplant. His sister, Anne, is a compatible donor, blood tests have shown that her kidney would be an excellent match, significantly better than one from a deceased stranger. Should Dan ask her to donate?

The surgery carries its own risks. If Dan makes the request, Anne would be required to respond and justify a possible refusal. His request would place a serious moral burden on her, one she may not want to bear. Whether Dan receives a suitable kidney would now, in a new and more personal sense, depend on her. She would be forced to engage with the decision, perhaps against her will. If she refused to donate, she would not only be denying the request but also taking on the emotional and moral weight of having done so. Dan may inform Anne, and other family members, about his medical condition and his need for a kidney without explicitly asking her to donate. By simply sharing this information, he makes her aware of his situation without creating a reason. If he were to make a request, Anne would then have a reason, though arguably not an obligation, to consider acting on it. However, out of respect for her interests and autonomy, Dan has a strong reason *not* to impose even that level of moral pressure on her by turning his need into a request she must seriously weigh.

6.3 When Requests Fail to Create Reasons

Sometimes you lack the authority to create a reason for action. When is this the case? Whether you have the authority to create reasons by making requests depends on various things. It depends on (a) the normative structure of the relationship the requestee seeks to have with the requester, (b) the social standing of the requestee, (c) the moral standing of the requestee, and (d) whether complying is good simply because you were asked to.

It is important to note here that you have the authority to make a request if you are able to create a pro tanto reason for action. Thus, you have the authority to make a request even if the reason it creates is ultimately defeated by conflicting reasons. For example, suppose that John asks Jill to read his manuscript over the weekend. However, Jill needs to work on a paper she must submit by Monday. Reading John's manuscript would place a significant burden on her. In this case, Jill's reason for not complying, rooted in her well-being, defeats the reason created by John's request. Therefore, she should decline. Her refusal would be justified on the grounds of protecting her well-being. However, John's request to read his manuscript still creates a pro tanto reason for Jill to do as requested. It is a reason to do so, even though Jill should not honor the request, all things considered.

However, in certain situations, you do not have the authority to make a particular request and should therefore refrain from doing so. This applies if any of the four conditions (a, b, c, or d) are not met. Let us consider this step by step. It is sometimes (a) your relationship with another person that provides you with a reason to perform a certain act if asked to do so. If your friend asks you to help her move house, you have a reason to do so.

But now consider this: suppose your neighbor asks you to discuss a marital issue with his partner. You are not a professional marriage counselor. Speaking to his partner might please your neighbor, as it reflects the kind of close, intimate relationship he hopes to establish with you. However, as the neighbor may be aware or presume, this is not the kind of relationship you want to have with him or with his partner. Nor do you want to assume the responsibility of helping solve their marital problems. This is something your neighbor should turn to a friend or a professional marriage counselor for instead. Of course, it is possible to have a relationship where discussing such personal matters would be appropriate. But as the neighbor may assume, that is not the kind of relationship you want to have with your neighbor. In contrast, if a close friend asked you to speak to their partner about a similar issue, you would have a reason to do so. Your relationship with your friend provides a basis for engaging in that kind of discussion. It may also be the case that someone should not concern herself with what you want her to do in certain circumstances. For example, John should not ask Jill to read his paper at her wedding. That is not the right moment for her to concern herself with John's paper, nor is it the right moment for John to bother her with it.

Someone might (b) have no reason to honor a request due to her social standing. Certain valuable features of actions do not apply to individuals who occupy particular social roles. Consider the following example: You, a staff member ask the dean to help you move house. You owe the dean a certain level of respect, specifically the respect owed to her social standing as a dean (see also McTernan 2023, 37). While her help might benefit you, her social position prevents your request from giving her a reason to assist. Therefore, you lack the authority to ask her for help in moving. Even though the requested act has valuable features, the request should not be honored by someone who has the social standing of a dean. Your request for help with moving creates a reason for a friend to assist, but not for the dean.

This brings us to the third reason (c) why we might lack the authority to make a request. You have no reason to honor a request that disrespects you as a person. This applies to requests that are, for instance, embarrassing, humiliating, or seriously harmful to the requestee. The requestee has no obligation to fulfill a request that would humiliate, embarrass, or seriously harm her. Such requests do not create reasons for compliance, not even weak reasons.

Furthermore, (d) it might be good for A if B does x, but it would not be good if B did *x* because A asked. Consider this: John's partner asks him to help with the housework. They agreed to share the housework equally, and she asks him to do his part every time she is about to do hers. She complains that he does not do his part without being asked. "I should not have to ask you; we agreed to do it together," she says. Their agreement already provides John with a reason to do his share. Does her request create an additional reason? John has a request-independent reason to help his partner with the housework, but if he does it only because she asked, he is doing it for the wrong reason. He should be doing it because they agreed to share the responsibility. The agreement itself carries the reason-giving force. If John acts solely in response to her request, he is not acting for the right reason. It is not good that he helps just because she asked. Therefore, her request does not create an additional reason; rather, it highlights an existing one. The request fails to create a new reason because it would not be good for him to act just because of the request—it would be good if he helps, but not if he did because she asked him to do it. John's partner should not ask John to do the housework. She rather has the authority to demand it.

6.4 Wronging by Requesting

Let us take a closer look at requests that are disrespectful to the requestee as a person (c). Nick Laskowski and Kenneth Silver argue that requests wrong the requestee when they are disrespectful to the requestee (Laskowski and Silver 2021). They illustrate the claim with the following example.

> «*Bar*. Stefan and Eva are old friends of means at their local bar, planning to tie one on as they usually do. Stefan happens to catch the attention of the

> bartender before Eva, so he orders the first round of drinks. Stefan then says to Eva, "I bought the first round—please buy the next one." (Laskowski and Silver 2021, 49)

Laskowski and Silver argue that it is wrong for Stefan to make this request. Stefan is "morally required to trust Eva … to reciprocate without being asked to do so" (Laskowski and Silver 2021, 67). His request is disrespectful, and therefore wrong. As such, it is a request that should not be made.

Whether requesting something is wrong or merely misplaced depends on whether Stefan is morally obliged to trust Eva and whether failing to do so is a violation of that obligation (see Laskowski and Silver 2021, 51). If Stefan is indeed morally required to trust Eva, he could be blamed for not doing so. The question is: Is Stefan morally obliged to trust Eva? If this were the case, his request for her to order the next round would not only be misplaced but also wrong. On the other hand, if no such obligation exists, his request would be misplaced but not morally wrong.

Laskowski and Silver argue that Stefan's request is disrespectful because he is morally obliged to trust Eva. This may be true. However, a request can be disrespectful for other reasons. Consider the case of asking someone to do something impermissible. For instance, Jeff asking Kate to help him cheat on a friend would be wrong, not because of a lack of trust, but because it is impermissible to ask someone to engage in wrongdoing. Therefore, requests can be wrong for various reasons. A request is wrong when it violates the requestee's right not to be asked for certain things. You have a right not to be asked to perform acts that are humiliating or embarrassing for you. Why? Asking someone to do something embarrassing or humiliating is an attempt to undermine their self-respect. Intentionally undermining a person's self-respect violates her moral right to self-respect. Imagine someone asking you to dance naked in front of your colleagues. Arguably, you have a right not to be asked to do such things, just as Eva arguably has a right against Stefan that he does not ask her to buy the next round, and Kate has a right against Jeff that he does not ask her to help him cheat. A request is wrong when it violates the requestee's rights. The reasons why someone might have the right not to be asked certain things can vary.

You have the right not to be asked to perform acts that are humiliating, demeaning, or embarrassing. You also have a right not to be asked to harm yourself—physically or psychologically. These rights are grounded in moral norms that govern how people should treat one another. No one has a reason to humiliate, embarrass, or harm themselves. Asking others to do such things is inherently disrespectful. Everyone has the right to be treated with respect, and any request that infringes on this right is morally wrong. Such requests are not only wrong but also constitute a wronging of the requestee. They violate the requestee's rights.

Therefore, the following principle applies to wrongful requests (WR):

> (WR) A request is wrong and a wronging of the requestee if and only if the requestee has a right against the requester not to make the request.

Wrongful requests should not be made and warrant blame. The addressees of such requests may rightfully complain about being asked. For instance, Kate not only has the right to refuse Jeff's request, but she could also justifiably complain about being asked to help him do something impermissible.

Requests are wrong if they are, in any sense, disrespectful to the requestee—whether as a moral person (c) or in relation to their social standing (b). However, not all requests that should not be made are necessarily wrong. For instance, your neighbor would not wrong you by asking you to talk to his partner about their marital issues. Such a request is misplaced because it does not align with the relationship you seek to have with your neighbor (a). Similarly, you do not wrong your partner by asking her not to leave you. Such requests may be inappropriate or misplaced without necessarily wronging the requestee. They are not disrespectful to the requestee as a moral person or in relation to their social standing; rather, they fail to create reasons for compliance because they either do not fit the nature of the relationship between the requester and the requestee or involve actions that should not be performed merely because they were requested.

In sum, some requests that should not be made constitute genuine wrongs, while others—such as asking your neighbor to engage in your marital issues—are merely misplaced without being inherently wrong. A request is wrong and a wronging when the requestee has a right against the requester not to be asked.

6.5 Not Leaving It Up to the Requestee

Requests also fail to create reasons for action if they are accompanied by threats. Consider this case: Jill asks her partner Paul to look after the children tonight. She adds, "Otherwise, I will ask our neighbor to come over and stay with the children." This would embarrass Paul, and Jill intends it that way. Her request is tied to a threat designed to embarrass him, putting pressure on him to comply. Does her request still create a reason for Paul to honor the request, or does the threat silence it? Paul may already have reasons, perhaps even an obligation, to look after the children. Jill's request could create an additional reason or obligation. But does her threat undermine the normative force of her request?

I think it does. Why? Requests leave it up to the requestee to decide whether or not to honor the request. Jill's threat ("otherwise I'll ask our neighbor"), however, seeks to take that decision out of Paul's hands. By threatening to embarrass him, she removes his discretion, which contradicts the nature of a request. A genuine request allows the addressee to weigh the pros and cons and make a voluntary choice. Jill's threat, however, gives Paul a reason to honor the request without further deliberation. In this case, it would be unwise for Paul to carefully consider the pros and cons. The reason provided by Jill's threat overrides other reasons that might otherwise apply to him in this situation. Jill threatens Paul because she does not want to leave the decision of looking after the children up to him. Her threat eliminates the discretionary element of a request, thereby undermining its normative force. A request should function as an invitation to act, not as a means of exerting undue pressure on the requestee. By imposing a threat, Jill strips the request of its discretionary normativity, making Paul's compliance no longer a matter of free choice. By saying, "Otherwise I'll ask our neighbor," she intends to take the matter out of his hands. Applying pressure to ensure compliance undermines the normative force of the request. In such a scenario, the requestee is not being asked to do something—she is being pressured into doing it, which is fundamentally different from a request. This holds even if the pressure is justified. Jill may have every right to pressure Paul to fulfill his obligations, especially if he regularly refuses. However, once she applies that pressure, she is no longer making a request. She may appear to be asking, but in reality, she no longer intends to give him a reason by asking. Instead, she creates a reason by threatening to embarrass him.

6.6 Deception

The validity of consent is often undermined by deception. If A consents to B doing x because A has been deceived by B about relevant facts concerning B's actions, then A has not validly consented to B doing *x* (see Dougherty 2013, 2018). But does something similar apply to requests? Do requests based on deception lose their normative force? Consider the following case:

> *Incompetent Jeff.* Jeff tells his colleague John that he is familiar with the debate that John's paper addresses. In reality, Jeff has no understanding of the subject. John, having no reason to doubt Jeff's claim, asks Jeff to read his paper.

Does John's request give Jeff a reason to read the paper? The normative force of John's request depends on whether Jeff would be doing John a favor by reading his paper. As I argued in the preceding chapters, a request creates a reason for action if doing as requested is good or at least not sufficiently bad and if it is good to treat the request as a reason for action.

However, since Jeff is incompetent with respect to the relevant philosophical debate, reading the paper would presumably be unhelpful for John, either by providing useless or even misleading comments or simply by wasting his time. Nor would it be good to take the request as a reason. John's request, therefore, does not create a reason for Jeff to read the paper. John's request would have created a reason only if it was good or at least not sufficiently bad for John that Jeff reads his paper, and good for him that Jeff takes the request as a reason. This does not hold in the case of *Incompetent Jeff.* Jeff's deception causes John to falsely believe he has a reason to ask Jeff to read his paper. If one has no reason to make a request, the request itself does not create a reason. John mistakenly believes that his request will create a reason, and this is how Jeff has led him astray. However, John's request lacks normative force *not* because

Jeff has deceived him, but because doing as requested has no valuable features. Requests grounded in deception do not create reasons for action, because if they did, they would not be grounded in deception. Deception induces false beliefs about such reasons, leading people to make requests they should not make.

Deception can also prevent someone from making a request that *would* have normative force. Consider the following case:

> *Competent Fred.* Jeff tells John that Fred is not familiar with the debate that his paper addresses. As a result, John does not ask Fred to read the paper. However, in reality, Fred is familiar with the debate and could provide helpful comments.

Had John asked Fred to read his paper, his request would have created a reason for Fred to do so. This would be the case even if John falsely believed that Fred had no understanding of the topic (for instance, if he asked him merely out of politeness). The request would create a reason because it would be good for Fred to read the paper and good for him to treat John's request as a reason to do so. However, Jeff's deception prevented John from making this request.

6.7 Summary

You have the practical authority to ask someone to do something if your request creates a reason (or an obligation) for the requestee to honor the request. A request creates such a reason if, and only if, it is good or at least not sufficiently bad to do as requested and good to take the request as a reason. In some cases, making a request can create reasons for the requestee to act. However, you should not exercise your normative power to create such reasons when the requestee is under no obligation to consider the request. You should especially refrain from making a request when the requestee has strong reasons not to fulfill it. In certain situations, a request does not create any reason at all, such as when the requestee does not want to engage in the kind of relationship that would make the request reason-giving. Additionally, requests may fail to create reasons if they are disrespectful to the requestee's social or moral standing. The latter holds for requests that are embarrassing or humiliating to the requestee. You have a right not to be asked to do such things, and making the request violates that right.

Requests also fail to create reasons when they are accompanied by threats. Applying pressure to ensure compliance undermines the normative force of the request. Deception makes requesters believe to have reasons to make requests they should not make. Deception may also prevent people from making requests that would create reasons for the requestees to honor the request.

7

Turning Down Requests

As I argued in the previous chapter, certain requests should not be made. This applies to requests for which there are decisive reasons not to honor them, to those that should not be taken as reasons for action, and to those that wrong the requestee. However, some requests do create reasons for action, and some even create obligations. While we often honor requests, we also frequently turn them down. But are we permitted to do so?

Raz argues that the requester intends to create reasons for the requestee to act, but these reasons are not, as he puts it, "conclusive" (Raz 1975, 83). As such, requestees are permitted to decline requests without thereby committing a wrong. The requester might feel disappointed if the requestee did not have strong reasons to turn the request down, but she had no grounds for complaint when her request was denied. Raz writes:

> A person who makes a request intends his making a request to be a reason for the addressee to comply with it. He hopes no doubt that his request will be a conclusive reason, but he does not intend it to be an exclusionary reason. If his request is turned down and he is not shown that there were sufficiently strong reasons to refuse his request he may be disappointed but he has nothing to complain about. Admittedly, his request was not complied with but it was considered in precisely the way he intended it to be. (Raz 1975, 83)

While you may rightly feel disappointed if your request is turned down without good reasons, it is—on Raz's view—always permissible for someone not to honor the request. This is how the discretionary normativity of requests can be understood: Requests may always be turned down.

7.1 Overview

In this chapter, however, I will argue that the discretion granted to the requestee should be understood differently. It is not the case that all requests may be declined. Rather, requests may be considered in light of all the reasons relevant to the requester's situation. For instance, when John asks Jill to read his draft, she is not obliged to immediately perform the requested act. Nor is she required to disregard her own reasons, such as those grounded in her self-interest. Jill might respond, "I will not read it over the weekend because I have planned to spend time with my partner." Taking such reasons into account is entirely reasonable, even if, upon reflection, the reason created by the request ultimately prevails.

When a request is turned down, you may feel disappointed. This could be a purely emotional response: frustration that the requestee did not do what you wanted. Things did not turn out as you had hoped or expected. Alternatively, you might feel disappointed because you believe the requestee failed to act as she should have, violating your normative expectations. These expectations might be reasonable, for instance, if you rightly believe that a good friend would have honored your request, your disappointment is warranted. Such disappointment may not be warranted if your expectations are not supported by reasons. Your request might have been unreasonably demanding, even for a good friend, and thus nothing she should have honored. Nonetheless, turning down a request might wrong the requester. This happens when the request creates an obligation that the requestee fails to fulfill. By declining the request, the requestee disregards their obligation, thereby wronging the requester. In such cases, the requester is entitled to complain. Disappointment and complaint differ: while disappointment reflects an emotional reaction, a complaint is warranted when the requestee violates an obligation created by the request.

Let us explore these issues in greater detail. The chapter is structured into four parts. The first part explores what it means for the requester to leave it up to the requestee to honor a request, discussing various interpretations of the discretionary nature of requests. The second part distinguishes between different forms of disappointment when a request is denied. The third part argues that in some cases, requesters may have grounds to complain if their requests are not fulfilled. The fourth part concludes.

7.2 The Discretionary Normativity of Requests

The discretionary normativity of requests refers to the leeway granted to the requestee in deciding whether or not to honor a request. This applies in situations where the requestee lacks a decisive reason either to honor or to reject the request. In such cases, the requestee is free to act based on the reasons that support honoring the request or, alternatively, the reasons that speak against it. As I argued in Chapter 3, a key aspect of this discretionary normativity is that the requester intends to leave the decision up to the requestee. But what does it mean *to leave it up to* the requestee?

The expression "discretionary normativity of requests" (see also Lewis 2018) suggests that it is at the requestee's discretion whether to honor a request. She may decline it if she chooses. But does the requester explicitly grant the requestee permission to reject the request at will? Is this what it means to leave the decision up to the requestee? What does it mean for compliance with a request to be at the requestee's discretion? How should this idea be understood?

I will present four interpretations of the discretionary normativity of requests and explain why each should be rejected. I will argue instead for an alternative view: that discretionary normativity of requests should be understood as permission to consider all relevant reasons that apply to the requestee. All reasons may be considered because requests are not intended to exclude reasons that speak against honoring a request from consideration.

a. Ignoring Requests

First, the discretionary normativity of requests could be interpreted as permission to ignore them, suggesting that requests do not need to be considered. However, they should not be understood this way. The requestee does not have a right to dismiss the reasons for and against honoring a request. She is only permitted to do so in cases where the request is not supported by reasons. However, when the requester has the authority to make the request, the requestee is obliged to consider it. Ignoring such a request would be disrespectful to the requester. For instance, if John asks Jill to read his paper, and she has reasons to do so, Jill must take those reasons into account. She may be justified to turn John's request down, but only after weighing the pros and cons of doing as requested. Therefore, leaving the decision to the requestee does not mean she may ignore the request.

b. Permitted to Turn Requests Down

Second, the fact that the requester leaves it up to the requestee might be understood as permission to turn down the request at will, even if the requestee does not have good reasons to do so. However, the discretionary normativity of requests should not be understood this way. While the requester does not intend to impose a duty on the requestee, this does not mean that the request can simply be refused. As I argued in Chapter 3, the requestee is sometimes obliged to honor the request. Whether she is obliged to do so is determined by the normative structure of the relationship between the requester and the requestee. The request might specify a general obligation the requestee has toward the requester, placing the requestee under an obligation to do as requested. In such cases, it would be impermissible for the requestee to turn down the request. Therefore, the phrase "up to the requestee" does not mean that the requestee always has permission to turn requests down at will.

c. Valuing Attitudes (Lewis)

Third, let us examine again Lewis's understanding of the "discretionary normativity of requests" (Lewis 2018; see also Chapter 3). As we have seen in Chapter 3, Lewis holds the view that the requestee has a reason to comply with a request only if she "places sufficient discretionary value" (Lewis 2018, 12) on the person making the request.

The request gives the requestee a reason only if she holds certain valuing attitudes toward the requester, and it is up to the requestee to adopt these attitudes. As I have argued in Chapter 3, the proposal faces difficulties if an alternative view is true according to which valuing attitudes only provide reasons if they are appropriate. More importantly, the account does not clarify what it means for compliance to be "up to" the requestee. If the reasons for honoring the request are provided by the requestee's attitude, then she lacks the freedom to decide whether to honor the request. For example, Lewis cites Anita's feelings of pity for Carrie. Anita cannot simply decide to feel pity; it is an attitude she either possesses or does not. It is not within her control to feel pity. What, then, is up to her in Lewis's account? To say that it is up to the requestee to do as requested must mean something different—something within her control. This provides a reason to reject Lewis's interpretation of the discretionary nature of requests.

d. To Choose the Reasons for Compliance

Here is another understanding of the discretionary normativity of requests. The idea that "it is up to the requestee to honor the request" could be interpreted as granting permission not to act on the reason created by the request itself. In other words, the requestee might be obliged to honor the request, but not necessarily because she has been asked to do so. For instance, Jill might have various reasons to read John's paper. She is not obliged to read it because John asked her, even if she acknowledges his request as a reason.

This understanding of the discretionary nature of requests assumes that we can choose which reasons to act upon. It would not make sense if we could not do so. If the requestee could not choose between acting on request-dependent or request-independent reasons, the notion of discretion would be meaningless. However, the challenge lies in the fact that—as I have already pointed out in Chapter 3—we do not seem to have the ability to select which reasons we act on. It might be good if Jill read the paper because John asked her, and John might hope that Jill acts on this reason, doing it for him. But the reasons we act on are not typically a matter of choice. As Scanlon correctly points out, we cannot simply choose to act for certain reasons. He explains:

> We do not … choose which things to take as ultimate reasons. We have to decide whether something is a reason or not … But deciding in such a case is not choosing, because it lacks the relevant element of free play … Holding constant one's judgment about which considerations count in favor of an action, there is no such thing as choosing, or "singling out," one of these as the reason that one is acting on. (Scanlon 2008, 60)

You act on a reason if you believe you have it. However, merely believing in a reason is a necessary but not a sufficient condition for acting on it, as weakness of will might intervene. Scanlon further writes:

> When one sees several considerations as counting in favor of the same action, one cannot choose to act on one of them rather than another unless one downgrades some of the reasons by changing one's mind about whether they really do count … in favor of the action in question … One can, of course, choose to bring about or try to bring it about that one regards or does not regard certain things as reasons … But what I choose in these cases is not to see or not see certain things as reasons, but to undertake a process of self-manipulation aimed at bringing it about that I have certain attitudes. (Scanlon 2008, 60–1)

If we are not able to choose the reasons we act on, leaving it up to the requestee cannot be understood as permission to choose which reasons to act upon when complying with a request.

e. Permitted to Take All Reasons into Account

Here is a more promising proposal of how the "leaving it up to the addressee" should be understood. A request does—unlike a binding order—not put the addressee under an obligation to disregard reasons that recommend not to honor the request. The requestee may consider the request in light of all reasons speaking in favor and against honoring the request. By contrast, a binding order is meant to be carried out without considering the pros and cons of the act. Consider the dean case again. Following the dean's order, I ought to chair the meeting of committee x this afternoon. I would much rather continue working on my paper. However, if the order is binding, I should no longer consider the reason provided by my desire to work on my paper. Instead, I should follow the order without deliberating whether there are stronger conflicting reasons, as doing so would be inappropriate.

This does not hold for requests. Requests do not exclude conflicting reasons. John contacts Jill and asks whether she would be so nice to read his draft right now. She was planning to have a drink with her friend Kate, which served as a reason for turning down John's request. Jill may still consider this reason, just as she would any other reason against honoring the request. Requests are not meant to exclude certain considerations from the requestee's deliberation. This is how "leaving it up to the requestee" should be understood: it grants the requestee permission to evaluate the request in light of all relevant reasons that apply to their situation.

This is true, even when you have an obligation to honor the request. It is still appropriate here to consider the request in light of all relevant reasons and verify whether you are truly obliged to fulfill it. If you reason correctly you will conclude that you should indeed honor the request. However, no one could criticize you for considering the request in light of all reasons applying to you in the given situation. As we have seen in Chapter 4, Owens argues that orders and requests do not differ in their role in shaping practical deliberation. If I am requested to do something, "it makes sense for me to do it ... without my weighing pros and cons" (Owens 2012, 86).

I think Owens is right, this might make sense in cases where it is obvious that there are no conflicting reasons. However, even in such cases, it would not be *inappropriate* to reconsider the reasons for and against it.

7.3 Being Disappointed

Raz argues that if a request is turned down in situations where the reasons are not sufficiently strong for doing so, you may be disappointed, but you cannot complain. Let us focus on the notion of disappointment. Is being disappointed an appropriate reaction when your request is turned down? To answer this question, it is important to distinguish between what Daniel Telech and Leora Katz call "propositional" and "reactive" disappointment (Telech and Katz 2022).

Propositional disappointment is a response to something you wanted to happen but did not. In this sense, you may be disappointed if a predictive hope or expectation has not been met—whether by other agents or impersonal events. Here are two examples of propositional disappointment:

1. John hopes that Jill will show up at his party, but she does not. John is disappointed.
2. Kate expects Brenda to visit her, but she does not. Kate is disappointed.

These are examples of what the authors call predictive hope and predictive expectation. John hopes that Jill will show at the party. This is a predictive hope. He hopes that something is going to happen. Kate expects Brenda to visit her. This is a predictive expectation. She expects that something is going to be the case. In the case of predictive hope, you believe that what you hope for is possible. In the case of predictive expectations, you believe that something is more likely than not to happen (Kate believes that it is more likely Brenda will visit than not). Telech and Katz write:

> Instances of propositional disappointment are impersonal in that they are directed toward states of affairs or propositions. (Telech and Katz 2022, 862)

In propositional disappointment, something you hoped or expected would happen did not occur. The object of this disappointment might be purely impersonal. For example, you might be disappointed that the sun is not shining today—you had hoped or expected it would be. Alternatively, the object of disappointment may involve other agents. John is disappointed that Jill did not show up at his party, he is disappointed by the state of affairs in which Jill did not attend. Similarly, Kate is disappointed that Brenda did not visit her. As the authors rightly argue, propositional disappointment is not warranted by moral failings but by unmet hopes or expectations. "I'm disappointed that he did not show up at my party because I hoped to see him," or "I'm disappointed that she did not visit because I expected her to come today."

On the other hand, *reactive disappointment* is a response to someone failing to meet a *normative hope or expectation* you held for her. Here are two examples of reactive disappointment:

a. Jeff expects his friend Jack to help him move. Jack does not show up, and Jeff believes Jack should have. Helping would be what a good friend does.
b. John expects Jill to read his paper, but she declines. John is disappointed because he believes that, as a good colleague, Jill should have read his paper.

In these cases, Jack and Jill fail to live up to certain normative standards—Jack being a good friend and Jill being a good colleague. Telech and Katz write:

> Reactive disappointment … refers to a type of disappointment that is essentially agent-directed and which evaluates an agent as failing to live up to

> a worthwhile standard or ideal, against the background of the disappointed's hope in the disappointee. (Telech and Katz 2022, 862)

Jack does not live up to the normative standard of being a good friend, and Jill does not live up to the normative standard of being a good colleague. Telech and Katz explain:

> In valuing our relationships and group memberships, we have reasons to act, attend, deliberate, and so on, relative to those relationships and group memberships, at least where these relationships and memberships are valuable—that is, worth valuing. (Telech and Katz 2022, 866).

And they add:

> Attention to our valuing relations reveals that we not only hold others to normative expectations; we also hold agents up to the evaluative standards and ideals governing our valuing relations. To hold others up in this way is to invest normative hope in them, hope for them to live up to values and ideals proper to our various valuing relations. (Telech and Katz 2022, 866)

Propositional disappointment is neither appropriate nor inappropriate because it involves no evaluative component. Disappointment can only be deemed appropriate if it holds agents to the correct evaluative standards and ideals. Propositional disappointment, however, does not hold anyone to normative standards and, as such, cannot be judged as appropriate or inappropriate. It is simply the emotional response of someone whose hopes and expectations were not met. This type of disappointment is made intelligible by referencing the person's unfulfilled hopes and expectations. Without this connection, it would not make sense.

By contrast, reactive disappointment can be either appropriate or inappropriate. It is appropriate if the underlying hopes and expectations are supported by reasons—in other words, if the requester has reasons to hope or expect the addressee to honor the request. A's normative expectation that B will do x is justified if A has reasons to believe B should do x as an act of honoring A's request. This expectation is justified not because A simply believes that B has reasons to honor the request, but only if A indeed has reasons to expect B to honor her request. A may sometimes have false normative hopes or expectations. For example, A might expect B to read her 500-page manuscript over the weekend, mistakenly believing this is what a good colleague would do. However, if A's request is not genuinely supported by reasons, A's disappointment with B ("I thought she was a good colleague, but I was wrong") would be unwarranted.

Telech and Katz view reactive disappointment as a form of reactive blame. It involves an evaluative belief that someone has failed to meet a certain normative standard. It may also involve a negative attitude toward the other person, becoming a form of affective blame. In any case, reactive disappointment entails a negative evaluation of what another person did or failed to do. The disappointed person does not need to conclude that the other committed a moral wrong but may simply believe they failed to live up to an ideal. For instance, Jeff may believe that while Jack was not obliged to help him, Jack nonetheless failed to meet the evaluative standard of how a good friend should behave in such situations.

A requester may be warranted in feeling reactive disappointment if her normative hopes and expectations regarding the requestee's compliance with the request are supported by reasons. A requester has reason to expect the requestee to honor the request if it is good or at least not sufficiently bad to do as asked, and good to take the request as a reason. Likewise, the requester has reason to expect the requestee to honor the request if she is obliged to do so. If the requester's hopes and expectations are indeed supported by reasons, her reactive disappointment is warranted.

Thus, we can state the following about reactive disappointment (RD):

> (RD) Reactive disappointment about a request being turned down is appropriate if and only if the requestee fails to live up to a valid evaluative standard or ideal.

It should be noted that reactive disappointment is only appropriate if the requester is justified in upholding the evaluative standard or ideal. This is not the case if, for example, the ideal is something that one could not reasonably expect someone to meet. The normative expectation must be supported by reasons.

7.4 Complaining About Turning a Request Down

Raz further argues that requesters may be disappointed if their request is turned down without being shown sufficiently strong reasons for the refusal, "but they have nothing to complain about" (Raz 1975, 83). However, there are cases where the requester has a right to complain when her request is rejected. This applies to situations where the requestee commits a wrong by refusing to honor the request—specifically, cases where the refusal not only fails to meet an evaluative ideal but also violates an obligation. If the requestee is under an obligation to comply, turning down the request constitutes a wrongdoing, justifying both complaint and blame. On the other hand, if the requestee fails to meet an evaluative standard or ideal, she does not commit a wrong .

For example, Jeff considers Jack to be a good friend, though Jack is not obliged to meet that ideal. A good friend might go out of their way to help, even when it is inconvenient, such as helping someone move house. If Jack fails to meet this standard, Jeff may be disappointed, but Jack has not committed a wrong—he simply has not lived up to the expectations of what it means to be a good friend. Jeff's disappointment arises from mistakenly thinking that Jack was a good friend, but no moral obligation was violated.

By contrast, failing to fulfill an obligation is a moral failing. For instance, if your partner asks you to look after the children and you are obliged to do so, refusing the request warrants not only disappointment but a complaint. Your partner has reasons to expect you to fulfill this obligation. Failing to do so is not merely falling short of an ideal; it is committing a wrong.

Raz seems to suggest that turning down a request never amounts to wrongdoing. This may explain his view that while you might be disappointed if your request is denied without being shown sufficiently strong reasons, you cannot complain, because turning down a request is never wrong. He argues that the requester does not intend to impose an obligation on the requestee. While this is true—the requester does not intend to impose an obligation—the requester can, as I have argued in the preceding chapters, still create an obligation for the requestee without intending to. When this occurs, rejecting the request warrants not just disappointment but a complaint from the requester.

The requester may complain that the requestee has flouted an obligation created by the request. Others may also blame the requestee for committing a wrong. In addition, the requester was wronged. The requestee had an obligation to honor the request, which corresponds to a right the requester holds against the requestee. Failure to do as requested, in such cases, constitutes a wrong done to the requester, a failure to fulfill an obligation, something the requestee owes to the requester, which warrants blame.[1]

Blame is warranted not only for failing to fulfill an obligation but also for failing to consider the reasons created by the request. As I have argued in Chapter 3, if a request creates reasons but not an obligation, the requestee is still required to take those reasons into consideration. She may ultimately reject the request, but only after giving those reasons due consideration. Ignoring them altogether is not permissible.

7.5 Summary

The fact that the requester leaves it up to the requestee whether to honor the request should be understood as permission to consider all reasons that apply to the requestee. Requests supported by reasons must be considered. Requests may be turned down (they also may be honored) if there are no decisive reasons not to do so. Requests should be rejected, provided the reasons they create are defeated by decisive reasons recommending not to honor the request. However, requests that create obligations cannot be turned down without committing a wrong against the requester. Requests that merely create reasons for action, or whose refusal reflects a failure to meet a normative standard on the requestee's part, may be turned down without committing a wrong. They may be turned down after having been considered. In some cases, turning down requests may evoke reactive disappointment when requestees fail to meet certain normative standards by refusing the requests. Refusing to honor requests warrants blame when the requestee has an obligation to honor the request.

8

Conclusions

Our investigation into the nature and normativity of requests is now complete. This is the account of the normativity of requests that I have argued for throughout this book.

I contend that we should prefer a normative view of requests over an epistemic one. According to the epistemic account, requests have informational but no normative content. They inform the requestees that the requester wants them to do or refrain from doing something. The requestees might already have independent reasons to honor the request. If this is the case, the request serves merely to draw the requestees' attention to the reasons they already have to honor the request.

I argued that the epistemic view is mistaken. Requests do not merely convey information; they have normative force in their own right. By making a request, you communicate the intention to create a reason for the requestee to do as requested. We want the request itself to serve as a reason for the requestee to do what we are asking, not merely to inform them of what we want. Wanting another person to do x does not necessarily imply asking them to do so. For instance, A might want B to do x but still say, "I'm not going to ask B to do x." This statement would make no sense if the epistemic account of requests were correct. A might refrain from asking B to do x because A does not want B to do x because A requested it. What we typically aim for when making a request is to create a reason for the requestee to act.

By making requests, we can create reasons and obligations for others. How this happens can be explained by referring to request norms. Request norms that take the form "If and because A asks B to do x, B has a reason to do x" grant us the ability to create reasons through making requests. Specifically, this norm holds if doing x is good or at least not sufficiently bad and good to take A's request as a reason for action. Similarly, how requests create obligations can also be explained by these norms. Some request norms express obligations, such as "If and because A asks B to do y, B is obliged to do y." These norms exist when a request invokes a general obligation that the requestee has toward the requester. For example, my partner's request that I look after the children tonight creates an obligation, provided that I have a general obligation to do my share in caring for our children. Whether I have this obligation depends on what I owe my partner.

Thus, what a request norm tells us to do depends on the normative structure of the relationship between the requester and the requestee. In other words, it depends on what we owe to strangers, neighbors, friends, relatives, and partners. We can create reasons for others by requesting them to do something for us, but certain requests may only create reasons for specific people. For instance, we may have reasons to help neighbors move, while we might be *obliged* to do the same for friends. In the latter case, turning down the request would be wrong, and the requester would be justified in complaining about the rejection. Turning down my neighbor's request would warrant reactive disappointment ("This is not what good neighbors do") but would not warrant a complaint.

We can create reasons to perform acts that already have independent reason-giving features. Our ability to create reasons for action comes into play when it is valuable to do so. Creating reasons is instrumentally valuable if and because it increases the likelihood that someone will do a favor for another. For example, if A gives B a reason to pass the salt by asking, A makes it more likely that B will pass the salt, which is desirable. The same applies to considering the request as a reason, as it increases the likelihood of acting out of respect for others' reason-giving authority.

Some requests, however, do not create reasons or obligations. This applies to requests that do not align with the normative structure of the relationship between the requester and the requestee. It also applies to requests that are incompatible with either the social or moral standing of the requestee. Furthermore, it applies to requests that should not be taken as reasons for action. This also applies to requests that wrong the requestee—such as those that are humiliating or embarrassing, thereby violating their rights. In such cases, requestees would be justified in complaining about being addressed in this manner.

8.1 A World without Requests

Imagine a world where people did not address each other by making requests. They are not familiar with this way of getting others to do what you want them to do. They rather do so by using other means, for instance, by threatening others or by offering certain rewards for doing what they want others to do. In this world A does not ask B to read her paper. A might threaten to harm B if she refuses to comment on her draft. A thereby provides B with a reason to read the draft. However, A would do so by wronging B. Alternatively A might offer B a drink for reading her draft. This would presumably provide B with a reason to act accordingly. However, in that case, B would not be acting for A but rather to obtain the mentioned benefit. While it might be beneficial for A to get B to do what she wants by offering B a drink, it would be even better if B did it for A's sake. B does x for A's sake if B does it because B was asked by A to do x.

Thus, in a world without requests, people would not be able to perform certain actions for others. Such a world would lack something valuable to us, namely, the ability to do things for others simply because they want us to, out of respect for their reason-giving authority. This is the value that complying with requests brings about. And it is precisely what we do when we grant favors just because someone asks us to.

Moreover, honoring requests has the added value of shaping meaningful relationships that might not have otherwise developed. Requests create opportunities for valuable future interactions and connections. Reading John's paper, for instance, might enable her to ask John for favors in the future, or it might mark the beginning of a personal relationship. Similarly, giving a stranger directions to the station might not seem valuable in itself (even though it might be valuable in its own right), but the next time a tourist asks for help, it could spark an engaging conversation about the meaning of life. In sum, the normative power we have to create reasons by making requests opens up the potential for valuable forms of interaction and relationships that we might otherwise never experience.

8.2 Remaining Doubts

Some readers may still doubt whether we have the normative ability to create reasons (and obligations) through requests. Are requests merely a way of expressing what we want others to do? If so, they would not involve any, as one might think, "dubious" normative mechanism by which requests create reasons. In this view, making a request simply informs others of our desires, without creating reasons for them to honor the request.

However, the normative force of requests is not mysterious. A's request that B pass the salt creates a reason for B to do so. The practice of making and responding to requests is governed by norms, which are grounded in the reasons we have for following them. If A asks B to pass the salt, B should honor the request because the norm holds: "If and because A asks B to pass the salt, B should pass it." Following this norm is valuable. The reason-giving force of requests derives from the value of the practice of honoring them. No mysterious force needs to be assumed. The idea that requests create reasons simply follows from the broader view that reasons are provided by values. There is nothing puzzling or inexplicable about this.

8.3 Respecting Others

Requests are essential for getting others to do what we want without imposing our will on them, leaving it up to them to decide whether to honor the request. A request aligns with the requestee's interests, allowing them to consider all reasons that apply to the requestee in a situation where she is asked to honor a request. Requests do not provide preemptive reasons for the requestee to disregard conflicting reasons for action. Instead, the conflicting reasons may be weighed alongside other reasons that apply to the situation. This is likely why requests are considered the most respectful way to get others to do something for you. Even when someone could issue an order, they might still make a request out of respect. For instance, an employer may ask an employee to complete a task instead of ordering it, as this demonstrates greater respect. By making requests, we avoid imposing our will on others and thereby treat them with the greatest respect. This is why the practice of making requests is so valuable and essential for living respectfully with others.

Notes

Chapter 1

1 An epistemic account of the normativity of requests is also defended by Laskowski and Silver (see Laskowski and Silver 2021).
2 See also Raz (2009, 14). James Lewis has a similar view: "A request is an attempt by an addressor to create and communicate a non-obligatory reason for the addresse(s) to perform an action" (2018, 2). Lewis thinks that the requester has the intention to create a non-obligatory reason for the requestee to do as requested.
3 Raz writes: "It is possible ... to tell a person that, while I would like him to do something for me, I am not asking and am not going to ask him to do it" (1986, 36).
4 This is what Lance and Kukla have in mind when they write: "The output of a successful request is that the target now has a specific sort of reason to do what was requested" (2013, 460).
5 Weltman writes: "But one main reason I would choose to request rather than wish in some context is that I want to increase the chances that you will X compared to if I were to wish that you would X" (2022, 21).
6 Giving consent does not necessarily mean that you desire the act you consent to. For example, I might consent to a colleague attending my party, even while hoping he does not come because I do not like him.

Chapter 2

1 Owens calls this "brute conventionalism," "according to which the mere fact that a rule is recognized in our community binds us all to conformity" (Owens 2022, 8).
2 see Kiesewetter (2022).
3 Bruno argues that, for instance, autonomy rights might be explained by appeal to the value autonomy has for us. The value of being able to decide how one is to live one's life seems "fit to ground reasons not to violate autonomy-rights not only through the disvalue that violations can have for the pursuit of individual plans, but at least also through the value that having the right itself has for an agent" (Bruno 2022, 3221).

Chapter 3

1 See also Benziman (2023, 299).
2 Lewis draws here from a longer discussion from Samuel Scheffler's "Equality and Tradition" (Scheffler 2010), see Lewis (2018, 6).
3 I will not argue for this view. This would be the topic of another book.
4 In Schaber (2021) I argue that all request-dependent reasons have the same weight. Weltman is right that we should reject this view.

Chapter 4

1 The obligations might be either moral or nonmoral. I will not address the question of what makes an obligation a moral one.
2 Consent has the same structure. The consent-giver intends to make something permissible and does this, as David Owens puts it, by communicating an intention of hereby making it the case that someone would not be wronged by performing the consented act (Owens 2012, 166). As in the case of orders, the consent-giver does not need to have the intention to release the consent-receiver from a duty. She just has to *communicate* the intention to do so.
3 You might have either a moral or a nonmoral obligation to do x. I will not discuss what it means to be under a moral obligation. However, what I say about obligations applies to both moral and nonmoral ones.
4 Practical authority has to be distinguished from what Raz calls "de facto authority." A has de facto authority over B if B follows A's orders without being obliged to do so (see Raz 1986, 26).
5 It might be better to call these communicative acts demands. A demands B to do x if A communicates that she wants B to do what B ought to do.
6 For a detailed discussion of Raz's account of practical authority, see Adams (2021), Darwall (2010), Hershovitz (2003), Hurd (1991).

Chapter 5

1 As suggested by Dan Khokhar in a private email.

Chapter 7

1 On directed duties, see Wallace (2019, 107).

References

Adams, N. P. (2021). In Defense of Exclusionary Reasons, *Philosophical Studies* 178, 235–53.

Benziman, Y. (2023). Do Me a Favor, *The Southern Journal of Philosophy*, 61, 297–307.

Bruno, D. (2022). Value-Based Accounts of Normative Powers and the Wishful Thinking Objection, *Philosophical Studies* 179: 3211–31.

Buchanan, A. E., and D. Brock (1990). *Deciding for Others. The Ethics of Surrogate Decision-Making*, Cambridge: Cambridge University Press.

Cupit, G. (1994). How Requests (and Promises) Create Obligations, *The Philosophical Quarterly*, 44 (177): 439–55.

Darwall, St. (2010). Authority and Reasons: Exclusionary and Second-Personal, *Ethics* 120: 257–78.

Dougherty, T. (2013). Sex, Lies, and Consent, *Ethics* 123 (4): 717–44.

Dougherty, T. (2018). Deception and Consent, in A. Müller and P. Schaber (eds.), *The Routledge Handbook The Ethics of Consent*, London: Routledge, 164–73.

Enoch, D. (2009). Wouldn't It Be Nice If p, Therefore, p (for a Moral p), *Utilitas* 21: 222–4.

Enoch, D. (2011): Giving Practical Reasons. *Philosophers' Imprint*, 11 (4): 1–22.

Franklin-Hall, A. (2023). Binding the Self: The Ethics of Ulysses Contracts, *Ethics* 134 (1): 57–88.

Gläser, M. (2019). The Normative Structure of Request, in Mark Timmons (ed.), *Oxford Studies in Normative Ethics* (Vol. 9), Oxford, 29–49.

Hershovitz, S. (2003). Legitimacy, Democracy, and Razian Authority, *Legal Theory* 9: 201–20.

Hurd, H. (1991). Challenging Authority, *The Yale Law Journal* 100 (6): 1611–77.

Hurd, H. (1996). The Moral Magic of Consent, *Legal Theory* 2: 121–46.

Hurd, H. (2018). The Normative Force of Consent, in A. Müller and P. Schaber (eds.), *The Routledge Handbook of the Ethics of Consent*, London: Routledge, 44–54.

Khokhar, D. (2022). Address and Response: The Normativity of Requesting, Begging, & Commanding, dissertation, University of California, Berkeley.

Khokhar, D. (2024). Begging & Power, *Philosophical Studies* 181: 1433–53.

Kiesewetter, B. (2022). Are All Practical Reasons Based on Values?, *Oxford Studies in Metaethics* 17: 27–53.

Lance, M., and Kukla R. (2013). Leave the Gun: Take the Cannoli! The Pragmatic Topography of Second-Person Calls, *Ethics* 123 (3): 456–78.

Laskowski, N. G., and Kenneth Silver (2021). Wronging by Requesting, in Mark Timmons (ed.), *Oxford Studies in Normative Ethics* (Vol. 11), Oxford: Oxford University Press, 49–69.

Lewis, James H. P. (2018). The Discretionary Normativity of Requests, *Philosophers' Imprint*, 18 (20): 1–16.

Lewis, James H. P. (2022). Relationality without Obligation, *Analysis* 82 (2): 238–46.

Marmor, A. (2011). An Institutional Conception of Authority, *Philosophy & Public Affairs* 39 (3): 238–61.

McTernan, E. (2023). *On Taking Offence*, Oxford: Oxford University Press.

Owens, D. (2012). *Shaping the Normative Landscape*, Oxford: Oxford University Press.

Owens, D. (2022). *Guided by Conventions*, Oxford: Oxford University Press.

Raz, J. (1975). *Practical Reasons and Norms*, Oxford: Oxford University Press.

Raz, J. (1986). *The Morality of Freedom*, Oxford: Oxford University Press.

Raz, J. (2001). *Value, Respect, and Attachment*, Cambridge: Cambridge University Press.

Raz, J. (2009). The Problem of Authority: Revisiting the Service Conception. In *Between Authority and Interpretation*, Oxford: Oxford University Press, 126–65.

Sayre-McCord, G. (2024). On a Better Moral Theory and a Theory of a Better Morality, manuscript, University of North Carolina. philosophy.unc.edu/people/geoffrey-sayre-mccord/.

Scanlon, Th. (1998). *What We Owe Each Other*, Harvard University Press.

Scanlon, Th. (2008). *Moral Dimensions*, Harvard University Press.

Schaber, P. (2021). The Reason-Giving Force of Requests, *Ethical Theory and Moral Practice*, 24 (2): 431–42.

Scheffler, S. (2010). *Equality and Tradition. Questions in Moral and Political Philosophy*, Oxford University Press, 15–40.

Shapiro, S. (2000). Authority, Public Law and Legal Theory, Cardozo Law School, Public Law and Legal Theory, Working Paper 024.

Tadros, V. (2016). *Wrongs and Crimes*, Oxford: Oxford University Press.

Tadros, V, (2020). Appropriate Normative Powers, *Aristotelian Society Supplementary* 94 (1): 301–26.

Telech, D., and L. D. Katz (2022). Condemnatory Disappointment, *Ethics* 132: 851–80.

Wallace, J. (2019). *The Moral Nexus*, Princeton University Press.

Weltman, D. (2022). What Makes Requests Normative? The Epistemic Account Defended, *Ergo* 9 (64): 1–19.

Weltman, D. (2023). How Requests Give Reasons: The Epistemic Account versus Schaber's Value Account, *Ethical Theory and Moral Practice*, 26: 397–403.

Index of Names

Index of Topics

www.ingramcontent.com/pod-product-compliance
Ingram Content Group UK Ltd.
Pitfield, Milton Keynes, MK11 3LW, UK
UKHW020208290926
15470UKWH00001B/59

9 781666 955361